£5. 00

NORFOLK RECORD SOCIETY

founded 1930

SURVEY OF
THE HOUGHTON HALL ESTATE
by
JOSEPH HILL, 1800

edited by
David Yaxley, B.A.

Norfolk Record Society
Volume L
1984

ISBN 0 9511600 0 1
Norfolk Record Society
Printed in Great Britain by Witley Press Ltd, Hunstanton, Norfolk

To the Dowager Marchioness of Cholmondeley

CONTENTS

ACKNOWLEDGEMENTS

I should like to acknowledge the kindness of the Sixth Marquess of Cholmondeley in allowing me access to the Houghton muniments and in giving his permission to publish the survey. The Dowager Marchioness of Cholmondeley has made me welcome on my many visits to Houghton, and her interest and enthusiasm have been very encouraging. Percy Baldwin has given me the benefit of his great knowledge of the Houghton estate as well as a great deal of practical help. Ian Dunn, Cheshire County Archivist, produced documents on the Cheshire part of Hill's work at the drop of a hat. I should also like to thank Gillian Beckett who, under less than ideal conditions, took many of the photographs used in this volume.

i. **Joseph Hill, Surveyor**

On the death of Horace Walpole, 4th Earl of Oxford, on 2nd March 1797, the Houghton estates of the Walpole family passed to George James Cholmondeley, 4th Earl of Cholmondeley, the grandson of Mary Walpole, Sir Robert Walpole's daughter. The property was extensive, and reputed to be worth £6,000 a year; but over the previous three decades it had been allowed to run down, and almost immediately the new owner commissioned a Cheshire surveyor, Joseph Hill, to prepare a detailed survey in order to have it valued. The survey was completed in 1800, and has remained a prized possession in the Houghton archives ever since.

Little is known about Hill's life. He lived at Malpas in south west Cheshire and may have been a relatively young man in 1797; a letter to John Stephens, the Cholmondeley agent, in that year is dated 'Houghton, Christmas Day, The Anniversary of my wedding', and in it Hill writes 'Am much rejoiced at what it has pleased Providence to send me since I left you, And am likewise happy, since things have happened well that I was so completely out of the Bustle'.[1] The birth thus casually mentioned was probably that of his eldest child, Jon, who was later to succeed his father in Lord Cholmondeley's service.[2] The Malpas register records the baptism of 'Joseph son of Mr Joseph Hill of Cholmondeley and Ellen his wife' on 29th August 1806, and in 1809 two other children, Charles and Helen, are mentioned.[3]

Hill was a man of many parts. He farmed as well as being a land-surveyor. In 1797 he sent directions to John Stephens concerning the management of his farm while he was in Norfolk, and in 1806 the rent for his farm was £84 15s. a year.[4] His cash account book, running from 1800 to 1814,[5] shows that he also acted as Stephens' assistant in the day-to-day running of the Cholmondeley estates in Cheshire, at a salary of £100 a year; his work included the purchase of bricks, paving flags, coal, lime, hair, victuals, quicksets, and a drum for the volunteers, paying out for thatching, ditching, felling, sawing, building, gardening, and molecatching, valuing timber, and receiving rents, heriots, and tithes. The account book also records many commissions for measuring and mapping private estates, at charges varying from 6d. to 1s. per acre plus expenditure on paper, vellum, and rollers for the map. He did considerable work for enclosure commissioners, measuring, mapping, setting out, and apportioning fields and commons. He was employed by turnpike trustees to examine the best direction for a new road, and by several incumbents to survey and value their tithes. One of the last big commissions recorded in the book is a joint survey, with Joseph Fenna, of Delamere Forest. This took place in 1812 and 1813, and Hill seems to have received £700 for his part in it, and an extra guinea for 'copying the map of Delamere on tracing paper for the use of Mr Harvey to explain to the Land Revenue Office what might be planted as next winter (a good Day)'. In 1813 he surveyed Lord Cholmondeley's Carmarthenshire estate for a fee of £172 10s. Nothing has been found to suggest how he was paid for the work at Houghton, but assuming that he charged his standard rate of 9d. an acre he would have received well over £600.

Hill may have begun his career as a surveyor in association with Joseph

[1] Cheshire Record Office (hereafter cited as CRO), DCH/AA Bundle 12.
[2] CRO, DCH S.16; DCH/X Bundle 11.
[3] CRO, DCH/1692.82.
[4] CRO, DCH/AA bundle 12; DCH/1692.82.
[5] CRO, DCH/1692.82.

Fenna, whose earliest surviving work, for the Tollemache family, is dated 1792-3. Hill's letters to John Stephens have a tone of respectful familiarity and equality, and it is likely that he had worked for Lord Cholmondeley before he received the Norfolk commission. His first surviving letter from Houghton is dated 23rd November 1797.[6] After commenting on his journey to Houghton and the 'vast deal of Company' there, including 'the Prince of Wales, the Stadtholder, Mr Fox &c.' he goes on: 'tomorrow Lord Cholmondeley goes to town till the 12th of next month when he intends bringing Mr Kent to value two or three farms in Massingham which I must get ready by that time if possible'. The reference is to Nathaniel Kent (1737-1810), who had been employed by William Windham in the 1770s to develop the Felbrigg estate and who, in 1794, had published *A General View of the Agriculture of Norfolk*; he was then a partner in the surveying and valuing firm of Kent, Claridge and Pearce. In spite of the weather being 'intolerable bad' Hill finished surveying Massingham in the week beginning 10th December, and between then and Christmas Day was employed in 'summing it up'. On Christmas Day he wrote to Stephens: 'Lord Cholmondeley wishes me before I return to survey Harpley and Castle Rising, there being much intermixed Land in the Former without any Landmarks which will I am afraid make it a tedious piece of business. The Time I expect to finish the above will I think be in about three weeks and longer in proportion to the goodness or badness of the weather'. Castle Rising, in fact, is not included in the finished survey.

The next surviving letter from Hill to Stephens is dated 29th November 1798. He had arrived at Houghton two days before after an 'exceeding indifferent journey'. After some discussion of the new lodges and gates (see below, p. 24) he writes 'I have not been well enough to stir out about business but hope to do a little tomorrow, the computed Quantity to be measured about here, is about 8000 Acres and supposing I measure 1500 weekly it will take me nearly 6 weeks, but shall in about 3 weeks time be better able to Judge'. On 12th December he writes 'I have been able to compleat full as much work for the present as what I expected but there will be about 4000 Acres that will be little less than six or seven miles off so that I must not expect upon a Average to compleat more than what I at first supposed'. Apart from Massingham, which he had already surveyed, only Dersingham and Syderstone, totalling 3,676 acres, approached this distance from Houghton. Towards the end of December snow prevented much work, but on 7th January 1799 he writes 'The Snow here is much wasted or rather shrunk down, so that it is not now above the shoe tops. I have made tolerable good progress this last week considering the badness of the walking'. Only one more letter from this period survives in the Cholmondeley archives, and it does not mention his work. The completed survey book is dated 1800.

None of Hill's subsequent surveys seems to have been as large or elaborate as the Houghton survey. It comprises well over 16,000 acres, and at his fastest rate the fieldwork must have taken a total of 11 or 12 weeks, while preparation of the volume, with its beautifully-written text, 18 finely-detailed maps, and 85 pen and wash drawings, must have taken at least as long again. This was at the beginning of a period of intense activity for land-surveyors. A vast number of their maps and surveys survive, but the Houghton survey is more extensive

---

[6]All the letters from Hill to Stephens are in CRO, DCH/AA Bundle 12.

than most, and the inclusion of a large number of illustrations sets it apart from the great majority.

It is not unique; two survey books of Tollemache estates in Cheshire by Joseph Fenna, the first of Wettenhall and Woodcott (1794-5) and the other of Alpraham and Tilstone (1795-8), contain 22 and 16 drawings respectively.[7] The estates are much smaller than those in the Houghton book, and the page size — $9\frac{1}{4}''$ by $6\frac{3}{8}''$ — is only a quarter of that used by Hill. Moreover, the whole arrangement of the Tollemache surveys is less spacious. The left-hand page of a typical opening has a short note on the lease, followed by a written description of the property. For example, of Rookery tenement in Alpraham, he writes: 'The Buildings are a dwelling House of Timber, partly nog'd with Bricks, or windings and Clay, plaistered over and Slated. (b). A Stable for 4 Horses, two Cowhouses for 12 Cows and a fother Bing: part timber and part bricks. (c). A small Stable for 2 Horses, warehouse and Granary over it: of Bricks, and Timber nog'd with bricks . . .' The page ends with a brief description of the soil, and sometimes a note of levies and taxes. The right-hand page is headed by a drawing of the property, set in an oval frame $4\frac{1}{2}''$ by $2\frac{1}{2}''$, with the viewpoint (e.g. 'S.W. view'), followed by a written survey that gives the name of the field, extent, value per acre in shillings, and the total value of the field. In the drawings, Fenna seems to have used the pen very sparingly. The outlines and many of the details of buildings, trees, hedges, and fences are in dense black, applied with a fine, sharp, rather dry brush; shading is in varying densities of grey wash, and only a few drawings have colour in the form of a pale yellow wash added to buildings and skies.

By contrast, Hill's main lines are much more free, cursive, and picturesquely irregular, particularly in parts like chimneystacks and the corners of buildings. He seems to have used the following stages:-

1. The outlines of buildings, and details such as doors and windows, are drawn freely in pale sepia-grey, sometimes with a pen, but often, as for instance in rooflines, with the point of a brush.
2. Dashes of light sepia or sepia-grey are applied to represent the textures of thatch and tiling, cracks and roughness in walls, and the like. Shadows are washed in with light sepia or grey.
3. Pale washes of local colours are applied:-

thatch:	yellow, probably raw sienna and raw umber, afterwards streaked with burnt umber. Some have a greyer tone.
tiles:	pale pink or brown pink wash
slate:	pale flat grey wash
walls:	mostly very pale brown pink, sometimes creamy pink, streaked and blotched with light pink and brown and grey. Flint walls are light grey.

4. Parts in shadow emphasised by grey or sepia wash.
5. Lines and details touched up in sepia with free, wriggling strokes of the pen; straight lines emphasised in sepia with pen or brush-point.

The ground is washed in with umbers, and grass is added in a light green; scribbled lines of burnt umber and sepia are added to give texture and for roads and paths. The form of bushes and trees is established with quick blotches of light grey-green or umber, and details and shadows added in blotches, dabs and scribbles of browns, greys and greens. A very light indigo wash is added for the sky. These are, in general, the methods used by eighteenth-century topographical artists to produce their tinted drawings.

In comparison with Hill, Fenna draws more delicately and carefully, and his sense of perspective and of the relationship between buildings is better than Hill's; he includes a great deal of the surrounding landscape, and his buildings are surrounded by convincing gardens, hedges, trees and fields, while Hill depicts no more than the yards, front gardens, paths, roads and ponds immediately adjacent, with a minimum of stylised vegetation. However, their treatment of details like thatch, slate, bargeboards, doors and windows is broadly similar, and it seems likely that Hill was influenced by Fenna, or at least aware of his work.

Brick was a major building material in both Cheshire and Norfolk. Fenna attempts to identify brick in his drawings by the use of fine, broken lines and vertical dashes, but without the accompanying written description many of his brick walls might pass for stone. Hill makes virtually no attempt, either in drawing or colouring, to differentiate between the many kinds of walling material in use, and in most cases only a study of his houses as they are today can identify the material. For example, he shows the walls of the farmhouses O.1 (Plate XXVI) and Q.1 (Plate XXXII) in exactly the same way, but in fact O.1 is brick and Q.1 is flint. In a few cases (Plates XXXI, LXIX, LXXIII, LXXIV, LXXV) he shows walls that are unmistakably of flint, but he does not use this convention for the walls of at least a dozen other houses that are built mainly of this material. Perhaps some of them, at least, were rendered and limewashed. Local quarried stone — carrstone, chalk and red rock — is not apparent in the drawings, although cracks in a few dilapidated houses suggest these materials, and some yard and garden walls appear to be built of large blocks of stone. One would expect carrstone to be used at Dersingham, but unfortunately none of Hill's houses in the village survives. There are six examples of timber-framed buildings; but in three of these the timber is exposed only by dilapidation, and it may well be that other cottages had hidden timber-frames. Evidence from the Medieval and Tudor periods suggests that timber building was common in the area. Roofing materials are more straightforward. All but three of the farmhouses have pantiled roofs, as have about two out of every five cottages. Most of the remaining cottages are thatched. Three farmhouses (Plates LVI, LXII and LXVIII) and four other houses (Plates LIX, LXVII and LXXII) have roofs that are indentifiable as slate — a fairly unusual material for the period.

In architectural detail, the keynote of the Houghton survey is variety. At least 25 types of mural windows, and a dozen types of dormers, are shown. The most numerous type of window, appearing in forty three houses, is an upright rectangle with a single mullion. Thirty houses, six of them large farmhouses, have long low windows with one or more mullions, but probably only a few of these (e.g. in Plate LIII) are true Tudor or Jacobean windows. Fourteen houses are fitted with typical eighteenth-century farmhouse windows, large upright rectangles divided by a mullion or mullions and a transom forming a latin cross. Only a few sash windows (Plates XLV, LII, LXXX and LXXXI) are shown, the rest of the windows, if they opened, being casements. There is a single example (D.3 Plate VI) of an apparently Gothick window. Two houses (Plates XXVIII and XLVII) are shown with diamond panes; the rest, where glazed, must have used rectangular panes of crown glass, perhaps in thin glazing bars that are not shown. Single side-hinged shutters appear on eleven houses, double shutters on nine, and drop-hinged shutters on two houses (Plates XXI and LXXVI) and a blacksmith's shop (Plate LXXIV). Eight buildings (Plates II, IV, XXVII, XXXVII, XLVII, LXVIII and LXXVI) have slatted windows, most of them indicating dairies. Most domestic doors are drawn as plain grey rectangles, but six farmhouses have rail and panel doors, and shed and outhouse doors are drawn with vertical planks, hinges, and handles. Chimney-stacks are generally of a late seventeenth-century or eighteenth-century type, corbelled or capped, but six houses (Plates XIV, LIII, LVI, LXIV, LXV, LXXIII) have shafts or stacks characteristic of the period around 1600. Chimneypots are conspicuous by their absence.

The apparent variety of house-plan is almost as great as the variety of architectural details. For instance, of the fourteen houses with a single central stack, no two have the entrance in the same position, and of the thirteen candidates for inclusion in the widespread 'three-cell' class of cottages or farmhouses with axial stacks, only seven (Plates XXXVII, LI, LV, LVIII, LX, LXV and LXVI) qualify, and most of these have detailed variations. In appearance the most homogeneous type is the cottage with a central door and single gable-end stack; there are, at most, ten of this type, and they appear to date mainly from the eighteenth century, although at least three (Plates XIX, LIV and LXIX) look earlier.

Dating the buildings simply from the drawings is not easy. Many of the surviving houses show 'dating' features that do not appear in the drawings; for instance, house L appears to be a standard, symmetrical superior cottage of the later eighteenth century, but examination of the building reveals blocked gable-end windows and two sets of fossil gables, taking it back well into the seventeenth century. Hill occasionally indicates straight joints (Plates VIII, XXXIII and XLIX) and blocked windows (Plates XLI and LXXII) but his approach is neither antiquarian nor picturesque.

Sixteen cottages are in obvious dilapidation or ruin, but he records their state in a matter-of-fact way that is one of the great virtues of the survey, both for the Earl of Cholmondeley and for the historian. Nearly a quarter of the cottages are shown in apparent disrepair, a proportion that is in accord with contemporary accounts of village housing. On the other hand, many cottages appear to be relatively modern, affording accommodation up to the standards of writers such as Nathaniel Kent and Arthur Young. Farmhouses appear to be well maintained, with decent outbuildings and barns. There are seven examples of 'winged' barns, with shallow projections on one side at either end (illustrated at Plates VII, XXXII and XL; on maps but not drawn at A.6, R.1, V.1, X.1), but only one representation of a porched barn (Plate LXXVII). Fences with stout posts and one, two, or three rails are common around farmyards, and there are also rail fences, mostly short, by cottages. Palings occur in thirteen drawings, most of them defining the front gardens of farmhouses and superior cottages. In at least two cases (Plates LXXX and LXXII) iron railings seem to be included. There are twelve varieties of large or farm gates, of three, four or five bars, and eight types of smaller gates. A few stone or brick walls are shown, but very few live hedges.

The maps, however, are full of hedges. They show a landscape in the last stages of transition from open fields to complete enclosure. In most of the maps only the remaining strips of glebe give a clue to the position and alignment of the furlongs of the open fields, but although most of the closes are the products of eighteenth-century enclosure and rearrangement, a number, as at Great Massingham, are based on the old pattern of furlongs, and in one or two cases, for example on Map 7, there is still a considerable amount of land in strips in 1800. The cartography is very fine, detailed, and delicate, and the maps are far superior to those in Fenna's illustrated surveys; hedges, trees, woods, roads, tracks, pits, commons, heath, pasture, arable, buildings and even a few prehistoric barrows are drawn with consummate skill and accuracy. The survey would be valuable for the maps alone; but the illustrations transform it into a document of the highest importance for the study of the history of Norfolk buildings and the eighteenth-century landscape.

ii. **The development of the Houghton estate**

The Walpole family, lords of the manor of Walpoles in the village of Walpole in the marshland of Norfolk, may have acquired Houghton as early as the twelfth century. They certainly had land in Houghton in 1286, and Henry de Walpol was lord of the manor in 1316.[8] It is likely that Houghton became the main residence of this family in the fourteenth century. Their possessions were not great; the will of Henry Walpole, made in 1442, mentions the manor of Houghton with its appurtenances in Harpley and West Rudham, the manor of Walpole, and the manor of Istead, in Weybread, Suffolk.[9]

The medieval manor-house may have stood between 50 and 100 yards north-west of the present house, at the north-east quarter of A.1 on Map 1. Flint walls four and a half feet thick were discovered here in the middle of the nineteenth century, one between 96 and 142 feet long aligned north-south, and another of unknown length running eastwards from it.[10] An inventory of Houghton manor-house of 1512[11] lists hall, parlour, 'drawt', buttery, kitchen, dairy, bakehouse, chamber over parlour, white chamber, red chamber, and four other chambers, all well, if not lavishly furnished. It was probably made in connexion with the will of Thomas Walpole, whose son, Edward (c. 1483-1559) made an important marriage with Lucy Robsart, daughter of Sir Tirry Robsart of Syderstone and aunt to Amy Robsart. This is probably the same house as that occupied by John Walpole, Edward's son and heir, at his death in 1588. His probate inventory gives the respectable total of £832, but this sum includes debts owing to him of £135 and farm deadstock and livestock, including 1,100 sheep, valued at £436.[12] The inventory mentions eleven ground-floor and five upper-floor rooms, mostly compatible with the rooms of 1510-12, but the furnishings are sparse. Perhaps John Walpole shared the house with other members of the family, or perhaps it was dilapidated and in need of rebuilding.

Five months after John's death in 1588 came that of the Earl of Leicester, lord of Syderstone and Bircham Newton for life by virtue of his marriage to Amy Robsart; these two manors, together with the lease of land in Great Bircham, passed to John's second son and heir, Calybut Walpole.[13] This was a

[8]W. Rye, *Norfolk Antiquarian Miscellany*, i. 273-4; *Norfolk Archaeology*, xxx. 273.
[9]Norfolk Record Office (hereafter cited as NRO), Norwich Consistory Court Wills, 180-2 Doke; the will is misdated 1462 in *Visitation of Norfolk in the Year 1563*, ed. G. H. Dashwood, i. 374.
[10]J. H. Broome, *Houghton and the Walpoles* (hereafter cited as Broome, *Houghton*), 1865, pp. 5-6; Mrs. Herbert Jones, 'Houghton-in-the-Brake', *Norf. Arch.* viii. 235-6.
[11]Cambridge University Library, Cholmondeley MSS (hereafter cited as CUL, Cholm.), account book 3.
[12]NRO, Consistory Court Probate Inventories, INV/4.10.
[13]NRO, Consistory Court Wills, 206 Homes.

substantial addition to the modest estate and could have provided the occasion for rebuilding the medieval house. Horace Walpole, writing in 1747,[14] stated that the 'old House', that is the present hall's immediate predecessor, was built by his great-grandfather, Sir Edward Walpole, supporting his statement by claiming that the ceiling of the yellow drawing-room of the present house was a copy of that in the dining-room of the old house. It is comparable, certainly, to ceilings of the mid seventeenth century, notably those at Coleshill. It should be noted, however, that Horace could not have known the old house at first hand, for although he was born in 1717, some four years before its demoliton, he did not visit Norfolk until 1736. Sir Edward was head of the family for only five years, from the death of his father Robert in 1663 until his own death in 1668. However, he may well have been in charge at Houghton for some time before his father's death. He was receiving rents for his father as early as 1653,[15] and an inventory of Robert Walpole's possessions in 1663 suggests that he was living in one room and had made over his furniture and estate to Edward.[16] Accounts for 1647-9 mention the sweeping of twelve chimneys at one time,[17] but hearth tax payments during the 1670s and 1680s are for twenty or twenty-one hearths, and in 1688, just before the tax was repealed, at least twenty-six hearths were paid for, suggesting a house rather larger than that of the 1640s.[18]

Whether Sir Edward Walpole re-built or merely extended the Hall at Houghton, he increased the ancestral estate through his inheritance in 1668 of extensive lands in Harpley from a cadet branch of the family. He was succeeded by his son Robert Walpole (the elder), a progressive farmer, who greatly 'improved' the estate as well as extending it by purchasing the manor of Great Bircham and an estate in Dersingham and West Winch — the latter from his cousin Valentine Pell. His son, Sir Robert, the famous statesman, added to the estate through the acquisition of the manor of Bircham Tofts and a substantial part of Great Massingham as well as consolidating the property through exchange or purchase in West Rudham. Thus, gradually, over a period of two centuries, a modest estate had been extended and consolidated (see map, Appendix I) into the substantial and reasonably prosperous one of well over 16,000 acres which is described in this survey.[19] It was this estate which provided the environment, albeit not the finances, for the magnificent park and Hall which Sir Robert Walpole built at Houghton in the early eighteenth century.

iii. **Houghton Hall and its park, 1700-1800**

Sir Robert Walpole succeeded to the property in 1700. Soon afterwards he began to modernise the old house, and undertook further alterations and improvements in 1716 and 1719.[20] Jonas Rolfe's letter to Walpole of 19th June 1721 graphically illustrates one reason why a new house was necessary: 'I am writing this in your Honours Study where I have a thousand ungratefull Companions the Mice; who doe dayly dispoyle to youre papers parchments &

[14]H. Walpole, *Aedes Walpolianae*, 1747, p. 48.
[15]CUL, Cholm. account book 7.
[16]Houghton Muniments (hereafter cited as Houghton), Red Box 1.
[17]CUL, Cholm. account book 7.
[18]Ibid. 15/1.
[19]For details of these acquisitions see Appendix III *sub* Maps II, V, VII, VIII, X, XI, XII, XIII, and XVI.
[20]J. H. Plumb, *Men and Places*, 1963, p. 136; *Sir Robert Walpole*, i (1956). 93, 273.

Bookes — especially those bound in vellum, which I could wish were putt up in Boxes or remov'd till some Fitter place might be fixed for them, the Vermin having nibled holes & made Free passage in to the drawers, they run in such numbers 'tis impossible to think of destroying them unless the whole be removed in the meantime what are yett untouched by them are very unsecure'.[21]

The decision to demolish the old house and to build a new mansion must have been taken no earlier than the late summer of 1720. In the previous year Thomas Badeslade was commissioned to survey Walpole's estates. He was paid two instalments of his fee in September 1719 and February 1719/20, and presented his final bill in April 1720.[22] This latter covers surveys and maps, both 'foul draught' and fair copy, of Houghton, Bircham Tofts, Bircham Newton, Syderstone, Chiplow Closes in Bagthorpe, and Dersingham, together with a 'map of Houghton Garden and Park made and finished over and above the other maps, and a perspective Draught of the House'. A similar survey and map of Great Massingham followed in 1730. The 'foul draught' map of Houghton[23] shows the park but not the house, but a map entitled 'A map of the Manor of Houghton in the County of Norfolk belonging to the Right Honourable Robert Walpole Esq', hereafter referred to as the 'fair copy' map, shows the plan of the old house.[24] It consists of two long parallel ranges running north-south and connected near their ends to leave a long narrow courtyard in the middle. The west front is some 130 feet long, the east about 150 feet, and each range is 20-25 feet in breadth. Running east from the north-east and south-east corners of the house are detached ranges some 90 feet long, and to the north stand four other detached buildings, probably barns, stables and animal houses. The whole layout looks rather earlier than c.1660. Unfortunately Badeslade's 'perspective Draught of the House' does not seem to have survived; it was probably a bird's-eye view like that of Chevening, Kent, drawn by Badeslade for Lord Stanhope in 1719,[25] and could only refer in 1720 to the old house. No picture of the old house, in fact, has been identified.

Preparations for building the new house began in the summer of 1721,[26] and the foundations were laid in May 1722. The original design was by Colen Campbell, but this was much modified by Thomas Ripley, Walpole's supervisor of building, by Walpole himself, and possibly by James Gibbs. A detailed comparison of the maps of Houghton shows that the new house stands immediately to the east of the site of the old house, and on the same axes. A drawing by Edmund Prideaux,[27] made between 1725 and 1727, shows the house and the south wing surrounded by scaffolding; the south-west tower bears a dome, cupola, and vane (dated 1725), while the north-west tower still has the pyramid roof that replaced Campbell's original pedimented design. Before the main west front Prideaux has a long building with a strange assortment of nine tall and two short windows on the ground floor, a steep-pitched

[21]CUL, Cholm. 898.
[22]CUL, Cholm. 23/1; Houghton, Red Box 1.
[23]Houghton, Map 2.
[24]Houghton, Map 1. Though neither signed nor dated, it refers to Badeslade's field book of 1720; it could be either the fair copy map or the extra map of the garden and park to which Badeslade refers in his bill, but for the sake of simplicity it will be referred to here as the 'fair copy' map.
[25]H. Avray Tipping, *English Homes*, period V, i. (1921) 13.
[26]CUL, Cholm. 898, 914.
[27]J. Harris, 'The Prideaux Collection of Topographical Drawings', *Architectural History*, vol. 7 (1964), 29-30, 72.

roof with eight dormers, and at least four chimney-stacks. The gable-end and stack of another building is shown against the west side of the north-west tower. Both buildings stand on the site of the old house, and although they are most likely to be purpose-built hovels for workmen it is just possible that they are the last, converted, remains of the old house. By 1727 William Kent had been commissioned to design the interior decoration, but the new house was still not finished when the Duke of Lorraine and Sir Thomas Robinson paid separate visits in 1731. Late in 1732 a fire in the cellar of the west front held up operations, and the masons were busy on details and internal alterations up to 1735, when the house was declared finished.[28]

The modernisation of the landscape for aesthetic purposes began after 1700. Colonel Robert Walpole, Sir Robert's father, was a progressive farmer, one of the first in north-west Norfolk to plant turnips as a field crop, and his account book includes a number of payments for dykeing and hedging from 1675.[29] It does not, however, make any mention of a deer-park, and the frequent entries of payment for venison suggest that there was no park at Houghton at this time. In 1709, however, Henry Bland, then rector of Great Bircham, wrote to Walpole 'Your Fawns drop very indifferently this year, almost all females'.[30] According to Broome, Walpole began systematic tree-planting in 1717, with A.39 and A.47 on Map I, followed by A.56 and A.57 in 1718.[31] Badeslade's 'foul draught' map of 1719-20[32] shows the park as an existing feature. 'The Breck by the Park Pale' stands just to the south of A.12 on Map I; there are belts of trees on the east, north, and north-west sides of the park, and although nothing is shown inside the park boundary the fact that a double avenue runs east from the main gate into the fields suggests that landscaping had already begun by 1719. An inscription inside the park on the 'foul draught' map gives the extent as 300 acres, but its actual extent could have been no more than about 225. Badeslade's 'fair copy' map[33] adds 62 acres of park and 20 acres of woodland, taking the park up to the Great Bircham boundary. This may account for the figure 300 on the 'foul draught' map. Much work on the park took place in 1720 and 1721. In August 1720 Kingsmill Eyre wrote to Walpole from Chelsea asking 'What forest trees you shall want from thise parts, because they are much sought for'.[34] On 5th June 1721 Edmund Cobb reported that the western part of the park was being paled; the 'Peice of New Parke' — probably the extension towards Great Bircham — was preparing for turnips; he had taken care to keep animals out of the 'Plattoones' (A.44, A.46, A.56, A.57 of Map I) and 'all the Groves'; and the gardener 'Wathers the young Plantations Constantly'.[35] Pales were still arriving at Houghton a fortnight later.[36] Walpole was concerned at the expenditure on labourers and weeders. The gardener, Fulke Harold, explained that during the last week in June fifty female weeders were employed in the new plantations 'or else they would have been nothing but weeds', while twenty nine men dug gravel, prepared ground for planting 'by the wall where the

[28]R. W. Ketton-Cremer, *Norfolk Assembly*, 1957, pp. 178-81; *H.M.C. 15th Rep. Appx. part VI, MSS. of the Earl of Carlisle*, pp. 85-6; Houghton, M.24.b.
[29]CUL, Cholm. 15/1.
[30]Houghton, Red Box 1.
[31]Broome, *Houghton*, 21-2.
[32]Houghton, Map 2.
[33]Houghton, Map 1.
[34]CUL, Cholm. 804.
[35]Ibid. 892.
[36]Ibid. 898.

new pales are seting down', hoed in the platoons where the women were weeding, and worked in the garden. He concluded 'the reson of such extroderny expense in weeding to the best of my knolege is the ground not being sofesintly plowed nor haveing time enough to kill the weeds'.[37]

By 1721 the aim of all this frenzied activity was to create a fit setting for the new mansion. However, the 'fair copy' map implies that the development of the park had originally been planned to enhance the old house. Two successive courts stand to the east of the house, and 40 yards further east a wide gate in a post-and-rail fence leads to an avenue 45 yards wide and some 300 yards long. At the eastern end of this avenue, at the top of a slight rise, is a formal embayed gateway flanked by high railings, obviously planned as the main entrance. On the other side of the public road is another railed embayment, and as on the 'foul draught' map the avenue continues into the fields for another 275 yards. North of the house is drawn a scattered, irregular grove of nearly 300 large trees, giving the appearance of old woodland but probably forming part of the scheme of planting. Against the north-west boundary of the park is a triangular plantation of about 30 acres, and belts of trees, averaging 40 yards in width, surround the park, with paling fences forming the perimeter. The park boundary measures three miles, and the old village, still intact, stands just outside its southern side.

Inside the park, sixteen formal avenues radiate from the old house and the garden to the park boundary. Immediately north of the house are gardens of about $2\frac{3}{4}$ acres, disposed in three rectangles; two contain fruit trees, and the third is apparently bedded. The main garden, containing about 16 acres, is near-rectangular and lies to the west of the house. A broad axial walk, formally defined by slim bushes, runs from an open grassed square next to the house to a semicircular bastion projecting into the park, and its line is continued westwards to the edge of the park by a wide double avenue. On either side of the walk is a wide verge, and a line of round-topped trees or bushes stands on a low bank. The north part of the garden is quartered by diagonal walks; each quarter is a dense grove, cut by serpentine paths that lead to openings in which are buildings, a statue, a mount, and perhaps a fountain. On the south side of the axial walk is a smaller garden, part of it a dense grove and part formally planted. The whole garden is outlined by a wall, ditch, or ha-ha that includes the western bastion and a smaller bastion on the north side at the junction of grove and fruit-garden. In 1731 the garden was separated from the park by a *'fossé'*.[38] The outline of the present garden is more or less the same as that on the 'fair copy' map, but the only solid boundary is the sunken north wall, of early-eighteenth-century brick and with a scar in the position of the bastion. The bank on either side of the axial walk is still visible.

The avenues may have been part of the planting carried out in 1721. If this is so, their appearance on the 'fair copy' map, which was probably completed by April 1720, implies that it contains a large element of forecast. This view is to a certain extent borne out by the fact that the 'foul draught' map, probably dating from 1719, does not show the western extension of the park and its avenues, although it does show the eastern avenue extending into the fields. However, it is certainly possible that some, at least, of the avenues were planted after Badeslade's survey and 'foul draught' of 1719 and before he made the 'fair copy' in, say, March-April 1720. A similar uncertainty sur-

[37]Ibid. 907, 904.
[38]*HMC 15th Rep. Appx., part VI, MSS. of the Earl of Carlisle,* p. 85.

rounds the garden. Volume III of Campbell's *Vitruvius Britannicus* was published in 1725, but the plates are dated 1723, and the text assigns the Houghton plans to 1722. Here the garden to the west of the house is very much the same as that on the 'fair copy' map, although the northern bastion is a simple semicircle instead of the more elaborate shape of the 'fair copy' map. Moreover, although the north wing with its oblong courtyard and parallel walk cover most of the fruit garden, the west ends of two of the fruit garden rectangles of the 'fair copy' map are shown exactly as on the map — in other words, the new house appears to have been imposed on an existing layout. The garden also appears on another undated, unsigned map at Houghton[39] which can be dated at the earliest to *c*.1723, as it shows the new house *after* the alterations to Campbell's original design, and at the latest to the first months of 1729 as it omits the new village. The main west garden is much the same in detail as that on the 'fair copy' and Campbell maps, but a square and a half of parterre has been attached to the south of the southern part, the axial walk comes almost up to the house, the northern bastion has resumed the shape of the 'fair copy' map, and the fruit garden has been almost completely obliterated by a plain parterre running the whole length of the west front of the house. Another 190 acres in the south-west and 90 acres in the east have been added to the park, giving a total of just under 600 acres. The area south-east of the house, including the church and part of the old village, still has its field hedges, but an avenue running diagonally through it demonstrates the intention to include it in the park. All the avenues of the 'fair copy' map are shown, and are extended into the additions. Outside the park, the Washmeres in Great Bircham is shown as a long serpentine lake, and pairs of rectangular plantations stand on either side of the West View at A.41 and A.45.[40] New roads run along the south and east sides of the park, giving it the shape that appears on Map 1 of the 1800 survey. The fourth depiction of the garden appears on an unsigned and undated plan in the Bodleian Library, which Willis attributes, on stylistic grounds alone, to Bridgeman.[41] The inscription to 'Esquire Walpole' puts it before 1725, and the fact that the new house is shown without wings suggests that the plan was made in 1721 or 1722, while Campbell was evolving his design. The general layout of the garden is similar to that on the other three maps, but whereas they differ from each other in a few details, the Bodleian plan differs from all three in a score of points, some of them major such as the whole layout of the southern part of the garden.

All four of the plans discussed above show a garden that has features in common with some of the contemporary gardens in which Bridgeman is thought to have had a great hand: Rousham in Oxfordshire, Stowe in Buckinghamshire, Scampston in Yorkshire, and Chiswick.[42] However, Chevening in Kent, a garden that appears to have no connexion with Bridgeman, has at least as many features in common with Houghton as any of the designs attributed to Bridgeman. Chevening was laid out about 1717 for Lord Stanhope, and drawn in a bird's-eye view by Badeslade in 1719 or 1720.[43] Walpole had quarrelled bitterly with Stanhope in 1717, but there was some sort of rapprochement in the first months of 1720, and in any case aesthetic

[39]Houghton, Map 23.
[40]According to Broome, the former were planted in 1717 and the latter in 1724: Broome, *Houghton*, pp. 21-2.
[41]P. Willis, *Charles Bridgeman*, 1977, pp. 86, 180, & pl. 81b.
[42]Ibid. 61, 66-8, 108.
[43]H. Avray Tipping, *English Homes*, period V, i. (1921), 13.

considerations may have transcended political disagreement. Apart from the doubtful Bodleian plan, nothing has been found to connect Bridgeman with Houghton at this time; and indeed Horace Walpole, admittedly writing some sixty years later, after describing the invention of the ha-ha, states: 'One of the first gardens planted in this simple though still formal style, was my father's at Houghton. It was laid out by Mr. Eyre an imitator of Bridgman'.[44] This is probably a reference to Kingsmill Eyre, who wrote to Walpole from Chelsea in August 1720; he sends lists of apples, asks for a plan of the orchard to be drawn by the gardener and for Walpole's requirements for forest trees, and adds in a postscript 'Standard Cherryes you shall want they are scarce of the best kinds'.[45] No other evidence of his involvement with the garden has come to light.[46]

In charge of the garden from 1718 at the latest was Fulke Harold, Herold, or Hurrel, who was held in such esteem by Walpole that his portrait hung in the breakfast room at Houghton. Until 1720 his house stood in the old village street; 'Mr Herold's house' mentioned in an account of 1734 was probably at A.6 on Map 1.[47] An account covering 1718-21 shows Harold receiving a total payment of £810;[48] no details are given, but the size of the sum, together with the letters of 1721 quoted above, suggests that considerable work was under way in the garden. In Edmund Prideaux's drawing, which shows the axial walk on the west side of the house much as it appears in all four plans of the 1720s, the slender columnar bushes on either side of the path are about nine feet high; small bushes alternate with round-topped trees some 18-20 feet high on the banks, and on the north side these trees are overtopped by the grove.[49] The accounts, maps and drawings together suggest that the garden was laid out not later than 1721 and possibly several years earlier. The theory that Pope had Houghton in mind as the model for Timon's villa in his *Epistle to Burlington*, though plausible, does not help to unravel the history of the garden. The *Epistle* was published in December 1731, by which time the garden was probably complete; but as far as is known Pope never visited Houghton, and even if he had seen the plan in *Vitruvius Britannicus* his description of Timon's garden is really quite unlike the layout depicted there.[50]

The development of the park in the south-east was obstructed by the old village of Houghton, which in 1720 consisted of sixteen tenements, including an inn and the vicarage, scattered on either side of the street west of the church. Both Campbell's map and the map of c.1723-9 show a reduction in the number of tenements, but the new village does not appear on any of the maps of the 1720s, and in the absence of firm evidence it must be assumed that the decision to build a new village was taken c.1728. The foundations for the first of the new houses were dug in July 1729, and the painters were priming doors and windows from 12th January 1729-30.[51] The New Inn (B.23 Map I) and Village Farm (B.1 Map I) followed in the next few years.

[44]H. Walpole, *Essay on Modern Gardening*, 1784, p. 53-5.
[45]CUL, Cholm. 804.
[46]In 1730 he corresponds with Walpole about a lawsuit over a Scottish mine, and in 1737 asks Walpole's help over his post at Chelsea Hospital: ibid., 1753, 1755, 1765, 1767, 2680.
[47]Houghton, Map 1; CUL, Cholm. 23/3.
[48]Ibid., 23/1.
[49]J. Harris, 'The Prideaux Collection of Topographical Drawings', *Archit. Hist.* vol. 7 (1964), 72; J. Cornforth, 'An Early Country-House Enthusiast', *Country Life*, CXXXI (1962). 536.
[50]Kathleen Mahaffey, 'Timon's Villa: Walpole's Houghton', in *Pope: Recent Essays*, ed. M. Mack and J. A. Winn, 1980, pp. 315-51.
[51]CUL, Cholm. 23/3.

Part of the old village site was used for stables. Badeslade's maps of 1719-20[52] show, in addition to any stables near the old house, three detached buildings called 'the stable for the hunters' on the village street and about 130 yards east of the site of the present stables. New stables, however, were being built in 1721, for on 5th June Edmund Cobb reported that 'Cornish' was being made for the stables, the roof was being framed, and the carpenter 'will put the Est End up Very Soone'.[53] Both Campbell's map and the map of c.1723-9 have a quadrangular stable due south of the new house and between the 'hunters' stable (which is not shown) and the site of the present stables. This quadrangle is undoubtedly what Sir Thomas Robinson saw in 1731: 'The stables (which are very large and [have] been finished about 13 years ago) are to be pulled down next summer, not only as they are very ill built, but stand in the way of one of the most agreeable prospects you have from the house'.[54] Robinson's account of Houghton, as will be shown, is not entirely accurate, and here he has got the date wrong. Three designs, with variations (e.g. cupolas instead of pyramid roofs on the corner turrets), appear in plans and elevations at Houghton.[55] All are for a U-shaped building with one long and two short sides. Straight joints at either end of the west front of the present stable block suggest that it was built with the west side largely open. Scars of pitched roofs at each end of the west and south fronts, together with the absence of the normal carrstone facing on the lower parts of these walls, indicate the presence of additional buildings, perhaps the 'New Leantoe Stables' mentioned in an account of late 1734.[56] The 'new' stables were being built in 1733-6.[57] The 'old stables' were still being repaired in November 1735,[58] but they must have been demolished soon after this.

Although Charles Bridgeman's part in the early history of the park is doubtful, he was certainly there in late 1731, for he is mentioned by Sir Thomas Robinson:

'The enclosure of the Park contains seven hundred acres, very finely planted, and the ground laid out to the greatest advantage. The gardens are about 40 acres, which are only fenced from the Park by a *fossé*, and I think very prettily disposed. Sir Robert and Bridgeman showed me the large design for the plantations in the country, which is the present undertaking; they are to be plumps and avenues to go quite round the Park pale, and to make straight and oblique lines of a mile or two in length, as the situation of the country admits of. This design will be about 12 miles in circumference, and nature has disposed of the country so as these plantations will have a very noble and fine effect; and at every angle there are to be obelisks, or some other building. In short, the outworks at Houghton will be 200 years hence what those at Castle Howard are now, for he has very little full-grown timber, and not a drop of water for ornament'.[59]

Robinson's letter is often quoted as a reliable description of Houghton at this time. He is not too far out in his statement of the acreage of the park, but the garden area, even including kitchen garden, buildings, and forecourts,

[52]Houghton, Maps 1 and 2.
[53]CUL, Cholm. 892.
[54]*HMC 15th Rep. Appx. part VI, MSS. of the Earl of Carlisle*, pp. 85-6.
[55]Houghton, A/36 to A/47.
[56]CUL, Cholm. 23/2.
[57]Ibid.
[58]Ibid. 23/3.
[59]*HMC 15th Rep. Appx. part VI, MSS. of the Earl of Carlisle*, p. 85.

could not have amounted to more than 30 acres; Horace Walpole, who came
to know Houghton well in the years 1736-45, wrote 'It contains three-and-
twenty acres, then reckoned a considerable portion'.[60] The lack of full-grown
timber was probably not as great as Robinson maintains, but it is certainly
true that Walpole had already planted on a generous scale. In addition to the
plantations of 1717-21, other totalling 132 acres had been made in 1724-7,
and another 54 acres followed in 1729-32.[61] The 'large design' shown to
Robinson has not been found at Houghton, but was probably similar to that
published by Isaac Ware in 1735.[62] This has features in common with
Bridgeman's work elsewhere, and displays the 'plumps and avenues' mentioned by Robinson, although the total circumference is eight rather than
twelve miles. It is not possible to fit Ware's outer belt to the actual landscape
with any accuracy, and although his plan was republished without alteration
in 1760 and 1784 only a few parts of it were actually carried out. On the maps
of 1800 only nine pieces of woodland[63] are in the position of Ware's rectangles, while three more[64] are woodland but of an entirely different shape.
Only the five plantations in Bircham Tofts, a small proportion of the whole
design, could have formed part of Ware's circumferential belt.

Robinson's comment about the lack of water at Houghton is similarly off-
beam. It is true that the pond by the stables was not there in 1731, as it was
formed after c.1736 on the site of the 'old' stables. Ware's map shows it as a
circle, but on two other undated maps of the 1730s it appears as an oval[65]. A
plan made in April 1749[66] gives the dimensions as 250 by 350 feet, and
locates 11 sink-holes broken within the pond and 3 sink-holes and 'a great
Crack in the ground' in the South Avenue near the pond. Lady Beauchamp
Proctor, visiting Houghton in 1764, commented 'Here is no water, except a
small bason near the stables, which has swallowed up an immense sum and
after all looks like a watering-pond, and I believe is used as such'[67]. The pond
lasted well into the nineteenth century, and the depression is still visible.
There was plenty of water at the Washmeres, a relatively low-lying place just
over the parish boundary in Great Bircham, where much of the brickmaking
for the new house took place[68]. Map I shows ponds at A.29, A.38, and A.41,
but manuscript maps at Houghton from the 'fair copy' map of 1719-20 on-
wards, as well as Ware's plan, show the Washmeres as a serpentine lake about
a mile long. However, bricks were still being made there in 1744, Washmere
Plantation was established in 1756, and it seems likely that this potentially
large lake was never integrated into the park landscape. In 1800 only the pond
by the stables and James' Pond (A.41 Map I) could be counted as ornamental
water. The pit by the church appears on the maps of 1719-20 and is probably
natural.

Ware's plan, and the two latest maps of the 1730s[69] show an intention to

[60]H. Walpole, *Essay on Modern Gardening*, 1784, p. 55.
[61]Broome, *Houghton*, 21-2. The plantations of 1724-7 were at A.44, part of A.49, A.13, A.14, Q.39, and the
unidentified Scotch Fir Plantation; those of 1729-32 were Q.41, the South Avenue, Q.19, and Q.33. Water was
carried to the garden and park from May to September 1730: CUL, Cholm. 23/2.
[62]I. Ware, *The Plans, Elevations and Sections . . . of Houghton in Norfolk* (1735).
[63]A.18, A.23, A.46, A.47, A.51, A.56, A.57, Q.39, Q.41.
[64]Q.19, Q.20, Q.22.
[65]Houghton, Maps 25 and 26.
[66]Ibid. A/57.
[67]R. W. Ketton-Cremer, *Norfolk Assembly*, 1957, p. 193.
[68]CUL, Cholm. 23/2.
[69]Houghton, Maps 25 and 26.

landscape the east view from the house by creating a splayed vista. A plan[70] dated 24th March 1737/8, shows the vista with four steps or ha-has facing east. Some earth has certainly been removed in this area, but the vista may not have been completed. The icehouse mound and five smaller mounds, appearing on Map I as round groves, were thrown up between 1742 and 1745[71].

There are no detailed plans of the garden layout in the 1730s, and Ware's plan, which shows the west garden as two solid groves divided by a wide walk, is obviously inaccurate. About 1745 a visitor reported 'We saw the Gardens which are not new, but neat and on the fore side of the house, the Park in which the first thing that presents itself to view is a fine Lawn, with a small Piece of Water in its center & 4 or 500 Head of Bucks upon its Banks. Beyond this Lawn are Woods pierc'd thro' with wide but short Cutts which make delightfull views from the house, all the Turff being exceeding fine Green like a Garden'.[72]

After the death of Sir Robert Walpole, then Lord Orford, in 1745, little seems to have been done to the park, since his son, the second earl, found debts of £40,000 and was unable to maintain his father's state. Apart from planting a cedar and pine grove in 1746 he did nothing. After his death in 1751, the garden and park deteriorated in the hands of his son, the attractive but feckless third earl. Horace Walpole, visiting Houghton in 1761, wrote: 'When I had drank tea, I strolled into the garden — they told me it was now called "The pleasure-ground" — what a dissonant idea of pleasure — Those groves, those allées, where I have passed so many charming moments, are now stripped up, or overgrown; many fond paths I could not unravel, though with a very exact clue in my memory — I met two gamekeepers and a thousand hares!' Horace is here recalling the years 1742-5, when he spent much time at Houghton as his father's companion. By 1773 things had got worse: 'Judge then what I felt at finding it half a ruin, though the pictures, the glorious pictures, and furniture are in general admirably well preserved. All the rest is destruction and desolation! The two great staircases exposed to all weathers; every room in the wings rotting with wet; the ceiling of the gallery in danger; the chancel of the church unroofed; the water-house built by Lord Pembroke tumbling down; the garden a common; the park half covered with nettles and weeds; the walls and pales in ruin . . . A crew of banditti are harboured in the house, stables, town and every adjacent tenement'.[73]

Horace inherited the title and estate on the death of his nephew in 1791, but he was then too old to effect any reformation. On his death in 1797 the fourth Earl of Cholmondeley, grandson of Sir Robert's daughter, succeeded to the estate. Map I shows the park as he found it. Some of the avenues on the earlier maps can be recognised: the North View, with its parallel and slightly earlier avenue; the South and East Views, and the West View outside the park; the beech avenue from the north-west corner of the garden up to and beyond the Water Tower, and traces of another going west from the same spot; traces of the avenues running south-west and north-west from the western bastion, and the avenue going north-east from that on the north wall. Although the bounds of the garden have changed little from the 1720s to the present day, the only surviving wall from that period is the sunken wall on the north side. Map I

[70]Houghton, A/53, A/54.
[71]Broome, Houghton, p. 11.
[72]Houghton, M.24.
[73]Horace Walpole's Correspondence, ed. W. S. Lewis, ix. 349; xxxii. 140.

shows palings on three sides of the park, the west boundary presumably being a fence. The ditch and bank of the northern boundary, heavily eroded, were visible in 1985 some fifty yards inside the line of the present park fence.

In the 1730s the main entrance to the park was between a pair of lodges opposite the New Inn, and there it remained until the change of ownership in 1797. Cholmondeley Hall, the family seat in Cheshire, was by then extremely dilapidated, and Lord Cholmondeley decided to use Houghton, at least until a new house could be built at Cholmondeley. Joseph Hill drew up plans of the 'Old Iron Gates' at Cholmondeley, and on 25th February 1798 John Stephens sent them to Lord Cholmondeley with the comment 'the ornamental part of the Pattern No. 1 is much shattered and very imperfect. No. 2 is what crossed the Court before the Hall Door, and seems quite perfect, and if your Lordship pleases may be immediately sent by the Canal to Gainsborough.'[74] It is not entirely clear whether these gates were the set made in 1695 by Jean Tijou or part of the extensive work of the 1720s by Robert Bakewell. New lodges were built at Houghton to accommodate the gates, but on 29th November 1798 Hill wrote to Stephens: 'Lord Cholmondeley is greatly disappointed in the Workmanship of his new Lodges, which are I must say the meanest looking Hovels of the kind I ever saw, but expect when he comes to fit the Gates he will be more and more out of Humour with them and do expect to see them pulled down and rebuilt'.[75] The problem of the gates continued, and on 27th December Hill wrote 'I received your letter last Night and can assure you have been in a terrible Funk ever since — if Mr. Pearson has cut them too narrow it must be owing to his misunderstanding me and not from any improper Directions of mine'.[76] He went on to give the exact dimensions. Map I shows the lodges, but whether they, or indeed the diminutive buildings there at present, are the 'hovels' or a rebuilt version is not clear. Also on the map but omitted from the illustrations in the survey are the church, refurbished by Sir Robert in early Georgian Gothick[77], the service and farm buildings near the Hall, the water-house, with its marvellous well 117 feet deep, and the Water Tower.

After the completion of Cholmondeley Castle the family was only intermittently resident at Houghton, and it is no surprise to find the estate offered to, and refused by, the Duke of Wellington. Much oak for shipbuilding, and walnut for musket stocks, was felled during the Napoleonic Wars, and in 1835 part of the park was ploughed up. James Grigor, visiting Houghton about 1840 wrote: 'there is not even a regular gardener kept . . . The gardens are gone, the lawn is obliterated . . . the entrance lodges, offices, and stabling, with their stalls for a hundred horses, are still here, but empty, — conspiring with other things to form a picture only of magnificent desolation'. Only the kitchen garden was kept up, being 'rather neat and trim'.[78] Later, the Prince of Wales visited Houghton and even considered buying it, but fortunately chose Sandringham instead. The plantations were expanded by both the first and second Marquesses of Cholmondeley, and the estate was again offered for sale in 1886, but remained unsold. It was left to the fifth Marquess and his wife, the present Dowager Marchioness, to restore the house and estate to much of its former splendour.

[74]CRO, DCH X, Bundle 6.
[75]Ibid., DCH/AA, Bundle 12.
[76]Ibid.
[77]Houghton, B/1 to B/14.
[78]J. Grigor, *The Eastern Arboretum*, 1847, pp. 192-7.

i.   The survey is bound in a single unpaginated volume, the pages measuring $19\frac{3}{4}'' \times 13\frac{1}{4}''$.

ii. Drawings and maps appear within the text, but in this edition they have been printed in separate sections. Their positions within the text have been indicated as follows:
Drawings. By placing the surveyor's property-identification code in square brackets at the point where the drawing appears, and by adding a plate-number for ease of reference, e.g. [A1. Plate I].
Maps. In the manuscript each map appears on the left-hand page at the beginning of that part of the survey which it delineates. It is keyed into the text under its title, e.g. [*Left-hand page*] The parish of Houghton [MAP I].

iii. The maps have had to be re-drawn in order to ensure the legibilty of certain features, notably of the code-numbers (e.g. A1 or 04) by which each piece of land and each building recorded in the survey is linked to the relevant map. Legibility has also dictated that a certain amount of detail be omitted, notably the names of owners of land which lay adjacent to the Houghton estate. Also, since most of the maps have a single alphabetical prefix to the code-number, this prefix has usually been omitted. Where this has been done it is clearly stated at the foot of the map.

iv. *Map conventions*

                       trees and woods

                       hedgerows

                       unhedged roads or tracks (yellow on original maps)

                       area of glebeland or other owner

                       pits and ponds (usually blue on original maps)

                       buildings (outlined in black and coloured red on original maps)

                       arable; all unhatched fields are pasture, common, or heath, indicated on the originals by wide-spaced grey stripes and irregular dots and dashes

                       demarks enlarged inset which does not appear on original map

v.   *Editorial policy*
The complete text has been presented together with all drawings. Maps have been re-drawn; 13 original maps are also included.
Editorial comment appears within square brackets.
Abbreviations have been expanded except in the cases of:

       do.   = ditto
       "   = 0
       A.R.P.   = Acres, Roods, Perches.

SURVEY OF ESTATES IN THE
COUNTY OF NORFOLK BELONGING TO
THE RIGHT HONOURABLE
GEORGE JAMES EARL CHOLMONDELEY
BY
JOSEPH HILL OF CHOLMONDELEY, CHESHIRE. 1800

[*Left-hand page*] The Parish of Houghton. [MAP I]

[A1. Plate I]

The Demesne Farm

			A	R	P
p 1st A	1	The Hall and Pleasure Ground	19	1	16
	2	Paddock	4	2	25
	3	Garden	7	1	36
	4	Carpenters' Yard	1	2	34
	5	Pightle	1	1	10
	6	Farm House Yard &c.	3	0	16
	7	Farm Garden	,,	1	6
	8	Park	450	1	15
	9	Paddock	10	,,	38
	10	Upper Do.	3	3	38
	11	Back Park	227	,,	30
	12	Sawpit Plantation	14	3	,,
	13	Birch Piece	7	3	18
	14	Twenty Acre	22	1	16
	15	Gravel Piece	35	1	26
	16	Do. Do.	29	3	,,
	17	Oak Wood Field	15	3	4
	18	Do. Do.	10	1	25
	19	Oak Wood Eighteen Acres	18	,,	,,
	20	Foxhound Grove	6	2	25
	21	Cover	,,	3	,,
	22	Town Plantation	14	3	38
	23	South Avenue	8	1	5
	24	Twelve Acres	12	3	20
	25	Seven Acres	7	3	20
	26	Eight Acres	8	,,	10
	27	Six Acres	7	,,	6
	28	Nine Acres	9	,,	20
	29	Washmeres	28	1	8
	30	Bircham Close	17	2	10
	31	Do. Do.	21	2	23
	32	Bircham Close	18	3	20
	33	Do. Do.	16	2	26
	34	Washmere eighteen Acres	18	,,	20

In the Parish of Great Bircham {30-34}

			A	R	P
35	Do. Do.		18	2	27
36	Brickiln Croft		8	”	25
37	Gamekeepers House and Garden		”	3	31
38	Pond		4	2	32
39	Carr Plantation		19	1	4
40	James's Pond Field		8	2	36
41	James's Pond		1	3	27
42	Carr Forty Acres		39	3	21
43	Killing Pit Cover		4	3	33
44	Middle Platoon		20	1	16
45	West Avenue	in the	28	1	30
46	Middle Platoon	Parish of	7	2	20
47	Open Plantation	Great	5	3	32
48	James's Ten Acres	Bircham	10	”	16
49	Three-cornered Piece		34	3	”
50	Black Brake		78	”	”
51	Bylaw Plantation		34	2	35
52	Bylaws		21	”	16
53	Do.		27	”	30
54	Do.		12	1	20
55	Do.		14	1	”
56	Upper Platoon		5	1	20
57	Do.		6	”	20
58	Old Common		290	2	”

		A	R	P
	Total	1784	3	15

Parish of Houghton

[B1. Plate II]

John Mitchell tenant

			A	R	P
Map 1st B	1	House, Garden, Yard &c.	2	”	34
	2	Pightle	1	2	17
	3	Home Field	15	2	29
	4	Houghton Field	19	1	8
	5	Swallow Close	18	2	16
	6	Elmer Close	13	2	34
	7	Do. Do.	14	3	”
	8	Do. Do.	15	”	24
	9	Rudham Brake	32	1	4
	10	Stile Brake	44	1	21
	11	Stump Close	9	1	4
	12	Lime-Kiln Brake	37	1	”

		A	R	P
13	Brockhall Way	79	1	35
14	Clay Pit Brake	37	1	19
15	Fox Cover Brake	25	,,	13
16	Brickiln Brake	28	,,	22
17	Forty Acre Brake	44	2	13
18	Engine Brake	49	1	33
19	Houghton Field	38	,,	,,
20	Roundabout	5	1	20
21	Bagthorpe Border	2	1	27
	Total	534	,,	13

[B22. Plate III]

| p 1st B | 22 | Houses and Garden's in Houghton Village | 4 | ,, | 30 |

[B23. Plate IV]

| p 1st B | 23 | The King's Head Inn, Garden, Stable &c | 1 | ,, | 35 |

Parish of Great Bircham

[*Left-hand page*] Thomas Rodwell's Farm [MAP II]

[C1. Plate V]

Thomas Rodwell
Tenant

2nd C	1	House, Garden & Home Close	25	1	20
	2	Home Close	18	2	6
	3	Lynn Drove	26	3	,,
	4	Forty Two Acres	43	2	,,
	5	Bylaws	12	1	10
	6	Do.	13	,,	30
	7	Do.	28	1	,,
	8	Do.	22	,,	32
	9	Do.	34	2	,,
	10	Do.	18	3	24
	11	Bylaw Heath Close	54	2	,,
	12	Heath Close	23	2	10
	13	Houghton Close	14	1	20
	14	Do.	24	2	20
	15	Do.	17	2	5

		A	R	P
16	Do.	20	2	30
17	Do.	24	,,	,,
18	Triangle Plantation	1	,,	32
19	Do.	2	,,	25
20	Common or Sheepwalk	80	,,	,,
21	Bircham Close	37	3	30
22	Crack's Close	34	2	20
	Road in Do.	1	,,	26
23	Do.	32	,,	15
24	Do.	31	,,	14
25	Home Sixteen Acres	17	2	5
26	Barn Yard &c.	1	1	27
27	Barn Close	15	,,	,,
28	Legg Common	37	3	10
29	Do.	81	3	,,
30	Great Brake	73	1	9
31	Heath Close	28	,,	23
	Total	905	1	3

Parish of Great Bircham

[*Left-hand page*] Edmund Holland's Farm [MAP III]

[D1 D2 D3. Plate VI]

Edmund Holland
Tenant

Map 3rd D			A	R	P
	1	House, Building, Fold &c.	1	1	33
	2	Cottage and Garden	,,	,,	34
	3	Do. Do.	,,	1	4
	4	Bells Close	18	2	35
	5	Knackers Close (exclusive of Glebe)	22	1	16
	6	Mill Close (exclusive of Glebe)	33	1	9
	7	Ganders Close (exclusive of Glebe)	13	2	24
	8	Eleven Acres Close	12	1	,,
	9	Fifteen Acres Close (exclusive of Glebe)	16	2	16
	10	Close by the Mill (exclusive of Glebe)	44	2	6
	11	Brash Brake	37	2	18
	12	Ransom Furlong (exclusive of Glebe)			
		2 Parts	39	1	2
	13	Gilberts Brake (exclusive of Glebe)	45	2	7
	14	Toadhole Brake	52	,,	12
	15	Home Twenty eight Acres (exclusive of			
		Glebe) 3 Parts	25	3	8

		A	R	P
16	Further Twenty eight Acres	28	3	,,
17	Claypit Close	33	1	5
18	Home thirty Acres (exclusive of Glebe)	30	2	24
19	Further thirty Acres	30	2	26
20	Near Sixty Acres	61	3	24
21	Middle Do. (exclusive of Glebe)	61	,,	,,
22	Further Do.	62	1	15
23	Peddars Road Brake	65	,,	,,
24	Pump Brake (exclusive of 20 Pieces of Glebe)	59	2	13
25	Barn Yard and Barn Piece (exclusive of Glebe)	21	,,	25
26	Barn Thirty Acres (exclusive of Glebe)	27	3	26

[D25. Plate VII]

[D27. Plate VIII]

| 27 | Bells House, Garden &c. | ,, | 2 | ,, |

[D28. Plate IX]

| 28 | Birds Cottage and Garden | ,, | ,, | 14 |
| 29 | Birds Pightle | 2 | 1 | 30 |

[D30. Plate X]

30	Another Cottage and Garden	,,	1	2
31	Queens Close	24	,,	4
32	Another Cottage and Garden	,,	,,	30

| | Total | 873 | 1 | 22 |

[E. Plate XI]

John Drage
Tenant

| 3rd E | House Shop and Yard | ,, | ,, | 13 |

Parish of Great Bircham

[F1. Plate XII]

William Knowles
Tenant

			A	R	P
Map 3rd F	1	Kings Head Public House Yard &c.	,,	2	1
	2	Orchard and Garden	,,	1	25
	3	Orchard Pightle	1	1	34
	4	Pightle	1	2	,,
	5	Do.	4	1	8
	6	Far Pightle	4	1	30
	7	Do.	4	2	8

[F8. Plate XIII]

	8	Two Cottages Gardens and Pightle	2	1	25
		Total	19	2	11

[*Left-hand page*] Martha Barker's Farm. Map 4th [MAP IV]

[G1. Plate XIV]

Robert Sparrow Tenant

Map 4th G	1	House Garden &c.	,,	1	18
	2	Frankmoor Meadow	2	2	2
	3	Meadow	1	3	28
	4	Vincents Meadow	3	,,	23
	5	Carris Pightle	1	2	,,
		Total	9	1	31

Parish of Great Bircham

[H1. Plate XV]

Martha Barker
Tenant

Map 4th H	1	House Building Yard &c.	2	,,	3
	2	Townhouse Close (exclusive of Glebe)	17	3	29
	3	Home Pasture	4	3	16
	4	Blacksmith's Pightle	2	2	15

[H5. Plate XVI]

		A	R	P
5	Blacksmiths House Garden &c.	”	1	4
6	Lower Yard	3	2	3
7	Home Close	9	”	37
8	Fring Road Brake (exclusive of Glebe)	11	2	17

[H9. Plate XVII]

		A	R	P
9	Townhouse Cottage Garden &c.	”	”	15
10	Garden opposite	”	”	13
11	Twenty eight Acres (exclusive of Glebe)	26	1	31
12	Thirty Acres (exclusive of Glebe)	28	2	10

[H13. Plate XVIII]

		A	R	P
13	Knackers House, Garden and Pightle	”	2	19

[H14. Plate XIX]

		A	R	P
14	Carpenters House Garden &c.	”	1	25

[H15. Plate XX]

		A	R	P
15	Shoemakers House Garden &c.	”	”	22

[H16. Plate XXI]

		A	R	P
16	Another Cottage, Garden &c.	”	”	30
17	Brickiln Piece	4	1	24
18	Greengate Pightle (exclusive of Glebe)	12	”	34
19	Crofts (exclusive of Glebe)	14	2	10
20	Greengate Brake	10	2	8
21	Do. Do.	23	3	”
22	Dudley Brake (exclusive of 3 Pieces of Glebe)	38	3	38
23	Snelling Stone Brake (exclusive of 2 Pieces of Glebe)	39	”	14
24	Blacksmiths Shop &c.	”	”	12
	Total	252	”	29

[I. Plate XXII]

George Batterbee
Tenant

4th I	Cottage, Garden &c.	”	1	24

[K. Plate XXIII]

Thomas Cawthorne
Tenant

		A	R	P
K	House Garden and Pightle	"	1	32

[L. Plate XXIV]

Mrs Blythe
Tenant

		A	R	P
L	House Garden and Pightle	1	"	17

[M. Plate XXV]

Lucy Kitton
Tenant

		A	R	P
M	Cottage and Garden	"	"	30
N	The Moor	4	1	12

Parish of Great Bircham

[*Left-hand Page*] Thomas Hebgin's Farm. Map 5th [MAP IVa]

[O1. Plate XXVI]

Thomas Hebgin
Tenant

Map 4th [sic; a mistake, as the previous map is Map 4, and the map of Hebgin's farm is numbered 5, which is also wrong, as the next map, of Lucy Kitten's farm, is also numbered 5. Hebgin's farm and its map, therefore, is here referred to as 4a].

O	1	House, Yard, Cottage, Gardens &c.	1	2	22
	2	Home Stall	6	1	27
	3	Pit Close	10	2	34
	4	East Field	35	2	26
	5	Burrow Hill fourteen Acres	17	2	"
	6	Do. sixteen Acres	19	2	7
	7	Do. eighteen Acres	18	1	38
	8	Do. twelve Acres	12	"	30
	9	Do. ten Acres	11	"	"
	10	Piece adjoining Cracks Brake exclusive of Glebe	23	3	6
	11	Lynn Road Brake	48	1	21
	12	In Glebe Close	3	0	2
	13	Piece adjoining Do	3	2	9

[O14. Plate XXVII]

		A	R	P
14	Upgate Pit Cottages and Gardens	„	1	„
15	Piece adjoining Cracks Brake exclusive of			
	Glebe	28	3	10
16	Cracks Brake	32	1	19
17	Steel Cross	32	3	4
18	Common Brake	22	„	12
19	Common in 2 parts	103	3	14
20	Backside exclusive of Glebe	54	3	13
21	Piece adjoining Tufts Road exclusive of			
	Glebe	13	„	22
22	Burnt House Close	18	„	3
23	Cottage Garden &c.	„	„	23

	A	R	P
Total	518	„	22

[O23. Plate XXVIII]

Parish of Bircham Tofts

[*Left-hand page*] Lucy Kitten's Farm. Map 5th [MAP V]

[P1. Plate XXIX]

Lucy Kitten
Tenant

			A	R	P
p 5th P	1	House, Garden, Yard and Pightle	2	3	23
	2	Barn Close	4	3	12
	3	Home Close (exclusive of Glebe)	10	1	34
	4	Docking Brake (exclusive of 3 Pieces of			
		Glebe)	18	2	15
	5	Do. (exclusive of 6 Pieces of Do)	17	2	28
	6	Newton Border Close	7	„	25
	7	Do. Do.	10	2	14
	8	Do. Do.	10	1	30
	9	Black Dyke Brake (exclusive of Glebe)	13	„	32
	10	Thirty Acre Brake (exclusive of Glebe)	28	1	31
	11	Long Brake (exclusive of Glebe)	23	2	19
	12	Brake adjoining Lowes Home Close			
		(exclusive of Glebe)	26	„	32
	13	Five Acres Brake	5	2	35

[P14. Plate XXX]

			A	R	P
14	Cottage Garden &c.		”	”	36
15	Hunger Hill		33	2	32
16	Burnham Brake		40	1	33
17	Do. Do.		46	2	13
18	Common		64	2	23
19	Bagthorpe Close exclusive of Glebe		30	3	37
20	Do. Do. (exclusive of Glebe)		22	2	13
21	Pit Close		11	3	26
22	Cottages Gardens and Part of Pond Pightle		1	”	”
23	The other Part of Pond Pightle	all in the	1	3	6
24	Far Pond Pightle	Parish of	3	2	10
25	Stocks Close	Great	18	”	”
26	Hockhams Close	Bircham	13	1	31

		Total	468	2	30

[P22. Plate XXXI]

Parish of Bircham Tofts

[*Left-hand page*] Thomas Lowe's Farm. Map 6th [MAP VI]

[Q1. Plate XXXII]

Thomas Lowe
Tenant

Map 6th Q	1	House Buildings Yard &c.	1	2	20
	2	Garden	”	”	34
	3	Home Close	6	3	33
	4	Peartree Close	20	3	33
	5	Bagthorpe Field	41	”	”
	6	Bagthorpe Brake (exclusive of Glebe)	39	3	32
	7	Long four Acres	9	1	20
	8	Spence Bottom Brake	33	1	”
	9	Black Ground	22	2	10
	10	Do.	32	”	8
	11	Jamesons Close (exclusive of Glebe)	37	2	15
	12	Two Acres	5	1	32
	13	Church Field	11	2	26

[Q14. Plate XXXIII]

14	Cottage & Garden adjoining Infield	”	”	25
15	Infield (exclusive of Glebe)	24	1	19

		A	R	P
16	Cuckow Hill (exclusive of Glebe)	52	2	12
	Road in Do.	1	,,	,,
17	Blackground Common	150	3	14
18	Oval Plantation	2	1	16
19	Tofts Hill Plantation	13	,,	,,
20	Tofts Dale Do.	34	,,	17
21	Field Barn Close	17	3	30
22	Twenty Acres Plantation	22	1	32
23	Lesser Fifty Acres	16	,,	37
24	Greater Do.	37	2	17
25	Cottage & Garden in Church Field	,,	,,	18

[Q25. Plate XXXIV]

[Q26. Plate XXXV]

26	Cottage and Garden in Church Field	,,	,,	18
27	Hall Barn Croft	2	3	30
28	Forty Two Acres	44	3	20
29	Swallow Pit	24	2	,,
30	Washmere Brake	38	,,	,,
31	Do. Do.	40	3	,,
32	Boxhill	16	3	10
33	Two Hill Plantation	5	3	16

[Q34. Plate XXXVI]

34	Cottage and Garden in Church Field	,,	1	,,
35	Forty Acres Brake (exclusive of Glebe)	61	2	24
36	Spence Bottom	24	,,	16
37	Point Cover	11	2	30
38	Point Close	21	2	18
39	Forty Acres Plantation	37	1	11
40	Cottage and Pightle adjoining Home Close	1	,,	,,
	Total	966	3	13

[Q40. Plate XXXVII]

41	Bagthorpe Point Plantation	3	2	10

Parish of Bircham Newton

[*Left-hand page*] Widow Blythe's Farm. Map 7th [MAP VII]

[R1. Plate XXXVIII]

Widow Blythe
Tenant

			A	R	P
Map 7th R	1	House, Garden, Fold Buildings & Pightle	3	ʺ	ʺ
	2	Piece opposite	ʺ	ʺ	14
	3	Town's End Pightle	4	ʺ	ʺ
	4	Dennis's Pightle	4	ʺ	7
	5	Do. Do.	3	3	36
	6	Near New Close (exclusive of 2 Pieces of Jas Claxtons)	13	ʺ	34
	7	Far New Close	9	ʺ	8
	8	Two Tree Brake	19	3	37
	9	Far Honey Hill Brake exclusive of 3 Pieces of Glebe	77	1	13
	10	Common Brake exclusive of Road	102	1	19
	11	Near Lodge Brake	53	3	ʺ
	12	Far Do.	93	ʺ	29
	13	High Park Brake	77	3	ʺ
	14	Cross Close	12	1	24
	15	Mill Hill Close	98	3	5
	16	Field Barn Close	16	1	ʺ
	17	Barn Fifty Acres	50	2	27
	18	Church Close exclusive of Road	37	2	21
	19	The Crofts exclusive of Road	18	2	34
	20	Do. exclusive of Glebe	16	ʺ	9
	21	Do. exclusive of Glebe & James Claxtons	16	3	24
	22	Fifty Acres exclusive of 8 Pieces of Glebe	38	3	ʺ
	23	Near Honey Hill Brake exclusive of Road & 17 Pieces of Glebe	53	ʺ	ʺ
	24	Clay Pit Brake exclusive of 7 Pieces of Glebe	49	ʺ	34
	25	Chalk Hill Brake exclusive of Glebe Roads and Claxton's Land	48	ʺ	ʺ
	26	Big Spot Lands exclusive of Glebe & Sparrows Land	67	2	18
	27	Little Do. exclusive of Glebe	20	3	20
	28	Cottage and Garden	ʺ	1	32

[R28. Plate XXXIX]

[R29. Plate XL]

	29	Farm House Yard &c.	ʺ	2	22
	30	Common or Sheep-walk	57	ʺ	ʺ

[R31. Plate XLI]

	31	Cottage & Lands adjoining Rectory	2	ʺ	28

[R32. Plate XLII]

		A	R	P
32	Cottage & Garden	”	1	”

[R33. Plate XLIII]

33	Cottage and Garden	”	”	10

[R34. Plate XLIV]

34	Cottage and Garden in Barn Close	In the	”	”	28
35	Barn Close	Parish of	8	3	20
36	Hockhams Close	Great	29	2	22
37	Tofts Close	Bircham	22	3	”
		Total	1128	2	15

Parish of Harpley

[*Left-hand page*] Thomas Herring's Farm in Harpley. Map 8th [MAP VIII]

[S1. Plate XLV]

Thomas Herring
Tenant

			A	R	P
p 8th S	1	House Garden Fold &c.	2	1	”
	2	Pasture	17	2	38
	3	Houghton Way (exclusive of Glebe)	12	1	34
	4	Rudham Way (exclusive of Mr Walker's Land)	25	2	7
	5	Elmer Field	31	”	13
	6	Elmer Close	5	2	2
	7	Clay Pit Pightle	”	1	35
	8	Carrs Pightle	3	1	4
	9	Houghton Field (exclusive of Glebe and Poors Land)	32	”	16
	10	Thirty four Acres (exclusive of Poors Land)	32	3	”
	11	Twenty five Acres	31	3	30
	12	Long twelve Acres	12	”	12
	13	Morgans Pit-hole (exclusive of Glebe)	24	3	28
	14	Nine Acres (exclusive of Glebe)	6	2	12
	15	Thirteen Acres and a Half	13	3	”
	16	Twelve Acres (exclusive of Glebe)	11	2	6

		A	R	P
17	In Hall Croft	2	2	”
18	Do.	3	3	32
19	Do.	6	2	”
20	Do.	1	3	28
21	Do.	1	3	5
22	Do.	2	1	”
23	Clay Pit Close	15	1	6
24	Three cornered Piece	18	2	20
25	Three Hills	21	”	10
26	Bassams Pightle (exclusive of Glebe)	9	2	”

[S26. Plate XLVI]

[S27. Plate XLVII]

		A	R	P
27	Pearsons House Garden Barn &c.	1	”	9
28	Pearsons Piece	7	”	20
29	Town House Piece (exclusive of Glebe)	15	2	”
30	Pains Eaves	6	”	26
31	In Harpley Dam Field	”	3	24
32	Do.	2	2	8
33	Do.	12	2	”
34	Do.	8	”	35
35	Do.	10	3	13
36	Do.	1	”	24
37	Do.	19	2	32
38	Do.	14	3	18
39	Do.	5	”	”
40	Do.	18	3	8
41	Do.	5	1	30
42	Do.	16	1	32
43	Do.	3	”	”
44	Do.	5	2	20
45	Do.	10	1	30
46	Harpley Dam Meadow	1	1	20
47	Blacksmith's House Garden &c.	”	1	13
48	Blacksmith's Pightle	”	3	16
49	Do. Do.	1	2	14

[S47. Plate XLVIII]

[S50. Plate XLIX]

		A	R	P
50	Overton Fox's House Garden and Pightle	2	2	34
51	Fox's near Pightle	3	3	23
52	Fox's far Pightle	6	0	6
53	Point Close	30	3	6
54	Long Fox Cover Brake	48	2	7

		A	R	P
55	Fox Cover Brake	46	2	28
56	Brake in Do.	1	1	20
57	Anmer Brake	31	2	,,
	Road in Do.	1	,,	,,
58	Hanging Brake (exclusive of Glebe)	41	,,	6
59	Long Brake	39	2	32
60	Upper Brake	39	1	10
61	Hawking Pole Brake	53	,,	15
62	Twelve Acres Brake	10	3	16
63	Common	166	3	,,

Total	1040	,,	13

Earl Cholmondeley

64	Point Nursery	11	3	6

Rose & Crown [S65. Plate L] Publick House

James Stapleton
Tenant

65	House Garden &c.	,,	1	30
66	Well Pightle	,,	2	10

[S67. Plate LI]

Thomas Gent
Tenant

67	Cottage & Garden	,,	2	,,

Parish of Harpley

[*Left-hand page*] Edmund Walker's Farm. Map 9th [MAP IX]

[T1. Plate LII]

Edmund Walker
Tenant

9th T					
	1	House Garden Yard &c.	2	3	28
	2	Pasture	8	3	29
	3	A Garden	,,	,,	26
	4	Piece adjoining Do.	,,	3	38

		A	R	P
5	Pightle	1	1	0
6	Rushy Close	2	3	3
7	Five Acres	5	2	32
8	Upper Sand pit Field (Exclusive of Walkers Land)	31	1	36
9	Another Part of Do.	,,	,,	11
10	Fisher's Brake (exclusive of Glebe)	25	1	6
11	Chapmans Piece	27	1	36
12	Sandpit Field	45	3	,,
13	Middle Brake	33	,,	12
14	Walsingham Way	31	3	,,
15	Lewis's Close	11	3	,,
16	Do. Do.	9	3	4
17	Church Croft	7	3	20
18	Another Part of Do.	1	1	13
19	Upper Pells	34	,,	30
20	Cottage & Garden	,,	1	3

[T20. Plate LIII]

[T21. Plate LIV]

		A	R	P
21	Pells Cottage &c.	1	2	32
22	Part of lower Pells	5	2	18
23	Another Part of Do.	,,	2	30
	Road in Do.	,,	1	3
24	Well Pightle	,,	3	,,
25	Pells Close	2	1	20
26	Town House Brake (exclusive of Glebe)	30	,,	,,
27	Lower Mill Field (exclusive of Poor and Walkers Lane)	33	2	20
28	Mill Brake (exclusive of Glebe)	22	,,	24
29	Fox Cover	7	,,	,,
30	Crosses Grave Brake	47	2	35
31	Great Brake	42	3	8
32	Upper Bearside	44	1	15
33	Lower Do. (exclusive of Savory's and Walkers Land)	42	,,	,,
	Road in Do.	,,	2	13
34	Piece in Town House Brake	,,	1	8
35	Town House Pightle	,,	1	36
36	Sandpit Close	7	,,	24
37	Sandpit Pightle	2	2	34
38	Brickiln Piece	8	,,	30

[T39. Plate LV]

		A	R	P
39	House Barn Garden Yard &c.	,,	3	6
40	Piece South of Sheepgate Way	3	1	15
41	Do. Do.	2	2	0

		A	R	P
42	Piece North of Sheepgate Way	1	2	6
43	Piece in Ravens near Limekiln Close	,,	2	12
44	Piece in far Lime kiln Close	,,	2	27
45	Do. Do.	1	,,	27
46	Do. Do.	3	1	18
47	Stingpit Common	2	,,	16
48	Sheepwalk	34	,,	,,
	Total	633	1	4

Parish of West Rudham

[*Left-hand page*] John Young's Farm. Map 10th [MAP X]

[U1. Plate LVI]

John Young
Tenant

10th U					
	1	House Building and Home Pasture	40	1	19
	2	Moor Piece	8	3	22
	3	Stackyard	,,	2	17
	4	Lower St Faize	63	,,	24
	5	Upper Do.	61	3	39
	6	Good Ale	35	3	34
	7	Sea Brake	87	1	13
	8	Water Cringle	130	1	26
	9	Near Massingham Close	27	3	26
	10	Further Do.	17	1	1
	11	Lewis's Close	18	2	14
	12	Piece in Edmund Walker's Chapman's Piece	,,	3	8
	13	Bonny Hill	15	2	37

[U14. Plate LVII]

14	Dye's Cottage and Pasture	3	2	17
15	Sixteen Acres	16	2	12
16	Long twenty Acres	19	,,	31
17	Common	7	2	38
18	Hundred Acre Brake	107	2	15
19	Woods Twenty Acres	20	2	17
20	Elmere Close	76	2	25
21	Cottage & Garden	,,	,,	18

[U21. Plate LVIII]

[U22. Plate LIX]

		A	R	P
22	May's Cottage & Garden	,,	1	30
23	May's Pightle	,,	3	8
24	Chequer Brake	90	3	12
25	Houghton Brake	101	,,	33
26	Burnham Brake	36	2	35
27	Houghton Fifty Acres	49	,,	30

[U28. Plate LX]

		A	R	P
28	Cottages & Gardens in Good Ale	,,	2	30

[U29. Plate LXI]

		A	R	P
29	Cottage & Garden	,,	2	35
30	A Garden where a Cottage formerly stood	,,	,,	6

Total	1061	2	32

Parish of Dersingham

[*Left-hand page*] Linghouse Farm. Map 11th [MAP XI]

[V1. Plate LXII]

Richard Stanton
Tenant

Map 11th V					
	1	House Building Yard &c.	3	3	7
	2	Barn Pightle	4	2	10
	3	Barn Close	11	2	8
	4	Twenty eight Acres	28	2	27
	5	Near thirty Acres	29	2	2
	6	Middle Do.	30	,,	4
	7	Peddars Road Close	34	3	32
	8	Burnt Herne	23	,,	22
	9	Three cornered Close	14	1	38
	10	Twenty four Acres	25	1	,,
	11	Eighteen Acres	19	1	20
	12	Sixteen Do.	18	,,	,,
	13	Rookery Close	28	,,	6
	14	Marlpit Close	18	,,	22
		Pit in Do.	,,	1	12

		A	R	P
15	Kitchen Close	16	2	20
16	Thirteen Acres	14	1	2
17	Coleseed Close	18	1	30
18	Near Field	76	3	25
19	The Field	143	3	,,
	Total	559	3	7

Parish of Dersingham

[*Left-hand page*] William Stanton's Farm. Map 12th [MAP XII]

[W1. Plate LXIII]

William Stanton
Tenant

ɔ 12thW	1	House Building Yard &c.	2	2	24
	2	Garden	1	,,	,,
	3	Clarks Pasture	8	3	25
	4	Hilly Pasture	21	2	15
	5	Dotshill Close	9	,,	28
	6	Candle Hole Close	18	,,	34
	7	Carr	2	,,	16
	8	Double Gate Close	6	,,	3
	9	Plantation in Do.	,,	2	36
	10	Snoringhall Close	15	3	17
	11	Osier Plantation	3	3	3
	12	Winding Barn Pasture	23	1	20
	13	Cock Piece	7	2	29
	14	Emletts and Pond Close	13	,,	25
	15	Wood and Wood Meadow	5	1	35
	16	Chalk Pit Brake	106	1	35
	17	Deal Furlong Brake	105	,,	32
	18	Shernborne Brake	81	3	10
	19	North of Shernborne Brake	22	2	32
	20	South of Anmer Road	28	3	4
	21	Plumpudding Bush	195	3	,,
	22	Dovehouse Close (held by lease under the Bishop of Norwich)	2	,,	22
	23	House Garden and Pightle	1	1	30
		Total	683	3	35

[W23. Plate LXIV]

[W24. Plate LXV]

James Yates

		A	R	P
24	The Cock Public House, Garden and Pightle	2	2	,,

[W25. Plate LXVI]

		A	R	P
25	Gay's Cottage and Pightle	2	3	3

[W26. Plate LXVII]

		A	R	P
26	Cottage and Pightle	,,	,,	30
	Total	5	1	33

Parish of Great Massingham

[*Left-hand page*] Anthony Beck's Farm, Map 13th [MAP XIII]

[X1. Plate LXVIII]

Anthony Beck
Tenant

			A	R	P
Map 13th X	1	House Buildings Yard Stackyard &c.	5	,,	22
	2	Rams Close	17	2	7
	3	Upper Do.	22	,,	,,
	4	Great Waltrops exclusive of Glebe	36	1	20
	5	Waltrops	16	3	,,
	6	Little Do.	11	1	32
	7	Three cornered Pightle	4	1	24
	8	In four Acre Pightle	2	,,	20
	9	In Hartswood Field	4	3	6
	10	Do.	4	1	16
	11	Do.	6	2	27
	12	Do.	3	3	16
	13	Do.	6	1	9
	14	Do.	1	2	4
	15	Do.	8	2	10
	16	Do.	1	,,	,,
	17	Do.	8	3	10
	18	Do.	,,	1	24

		A	R	P
19	Do.	1	2	26
20	Do.	4	1	32
21	Do. the Pightle	12	3	30
22	In Greeway Field	3	2	38
23	Do.	3	2	21
24	Do.	1	1	18
25	Do.	,,	2	35
26	Do.	7	,,	12
27	Do.	7	3	,,
28	Do.	5	,,	,,
29	Do.	,,	2	17
30	Do.	10	3	28
31	Do.	,,	3	24
32	In Greyton Field	9	,,	28
33	In Guyton Field	,,	2	10
34	Lynn Field exclusive of Glebe and Ravens land	27	5	24
35	Two Pieces adjoining Do.	4	2	13
36	Long Jackleys	27	1	,,
37	Do.	32	,,	,,
38	Twenty Acres Jackleys	20	1	16
39	Eight Acres Do.	8	2	34
40	Ten Acres Do.	10	1	10
41	Gilpars	23	1	8
42	Do.	25	1	28
43	Stonepit Brake exclusive of Roads	86	,,	,,
44	Well Hall Brake	43	,,	,,
45	Lynn Way	127	,,	4
46	Late ·Banks's Rams Head Close	4	3	27
47	Guyton Brakes	167	,,	,,
48	Guyton Fox Cover	11	2	12
49	Bean Ling Common	112	3	20
50	Grimston Bottom Common	204	,,	,,
51	Church Close	20	1	4
52	Cottage and Garden	,,	1	,,
	Total	1189	1	6

[X52. Plate LXIX]

Dr Reynolds Tenant

66	Late Bewleys Cottage and Garden	,,	2	,,
67	Part of Pightle	3	1	8
68	Little Massingham Close	6	2	14
	Total	10	1	22

[X65. Plate LXX]

		A	R	P
65	Thomas Muir a Cottage and Garden	″	″	16

[X61 X64. Plate LXXI]

Thomas Mason & John Jacks

		A	R	P
61	The Fox Publick House and Garden	″	1	4
62	Cottage and Pightle	″	3	27
63	Church Close	15	″	″
64	Jacks House Smith's Shop & Garden	″	1	20
	Total	16	2	11

[X53. Plate LXXII]

John Gage

		A	R	P
53	The Swan Inn Yard &c.	2	1	″
54	Swan Pightle	2	1	16

[X55. Plate LXXIII]

		A	R	P
55	Late Baxter's House Garden & Pightle	1	1	30

[X56. Plate LXXIV]

		A	R	P
56	Blacksmith's Do.	1	0	16
57	Wacey's Pightle	3	2	16
58	Church Close	12	″	″
59	Three cornered Pightle	4	2	″
60	Home Pightle	1	″	20
	Total	28	1	18

[X69. Plate LXXV]

John Curtis

		A	R	P
69	House Shop and Garden	″	1	″
70	Bullards	18	1	2
71	Little Massingham Close	13	2	32
72	Cottage and Garden	″	2	20
	Total	32	3	14

[X72. Plate LXXVI]

Parish of Great Massingham

[*Left-hand page*] William Banks senior's Farm. Map 14th [MAP XIV]

[Y1. Plate LXXVII]

William Banks senior
Tenant

			A	R	P
14th Y	1	House Building & Pasture	4	3	24
	2	Home Close	16	3	8
	3	In Hern Field	"	3	"
	4	Do.	1	2	7
	5	Do.	1	2	10
	6	Lynn Road Close	9	1	36
	7	Pit hole Close exclusive of Glebe	11	3	8
	8	Clark's Lane	3	3	34
	9	Knacker's Land	8	3	13
	10	Three cornered Close exclusive of Glebe	12	3	18
	11	Three cornered Pightle exclusive of 2 Pieces of Glebe	2	3	9
	12	Upper Broom Close	10	3	27
	13	Swan Field exclusive of 3 Pieces of Glebe	32	3	13
	14	Lower Broom Close	9	1	30
	15	Stubbs Pightle	2	1	30
	16	Sky Close	7	1	"
	17	In Brickiln Field	"	3	30
	18	Do.	2	"	4
	19	Do.	1	1	33
	20	Brickiln Croft	1	2	14
	21	Clements Hill exclusive of Glebe	8	3	"
	22	Roastmeat Land	3	3	"
	23	Whit Post Close	17	2	30
	24	Three cornered Piece	4	"	24
	25	Several	7	"	"
	26	Do.	3	2	34
	27	Barn Barn Yard & Brake	33	"	"
	28	Brickiln Brake exclusive of Road	49	2	20
	29	Cottages and Gardens	"	2	26

[Y30. Plate LXXVIII]

			A	R	P
	30	Cottage and Garden	"	3	10
	31	Foxhill Several	10	"	"

		A	R	P
32	Several	7	2	20
33	Long Brake	18	3	10
34	Lower seventeen Acres	16	2	20
35	Three cornered Brake	28	1	19
36	High Common	282	3	26
37	Lynn Lane Close	7	1	20
	Total	673	,,	7

Parish of Great Massingham

[*Left-hand page*] William Banks junior's Farm. Map 15th [MAP XV]

[Z1. Plate LXXIX]

William Banks Junior
Tenant

Map 15thZ	1	House Building Yard and Pightle	7	3	,,
	2	Town House Close	13	2	8
	3	Hand Field	12	,,	12
	4	Home Close	13	1	34
	5	Mill Hill	9	2	10
	6	Near Castle Acre Close	9	3	30
	7	Middle Do. exclusive of Glebe	6	2	8
	8	Upper Sky Close	10	1	,,
	9	In Townland Close	4	1	24
	10	Do. Do.	,,	3	33
	11	Castle Acre Close exclusive of Glebe	7	1	35
	12	Norwich Road Close exclusive of Glebe	12	3	20
	13	Piece in Brickiln Field	1	1	4
	14	Do. Do.	1	,,	32
	15	Do. Do.	1	3	4
	16	Lime Kiln Brake exclusive of Roads	46	3	22
	17	Several	6	,,	15
	18	Castle Acre Brake exclusive of Roads	129	,,	,,
	19	Three cornered Brake	8	3	27
	20	Upper seventeen Acres	17	2	8
	21	Fox Cover	12	3	33
	22	Common	150	,,	,,
	23	Near New Close	18	1	16
	24	Middle Do.	20	1	10
	25	Further Do.	16	2	16
	26	Beldram	12	0	18
	27	Claypit Close exclusive of Mr. Blythes	15	1	23

		A	R	P
28	Near Finchams exclusive of 3 Pieces of			
	Glebe	8	2	1
29	Piece in further Parsons hole Furlong	,,	3	,,
30	Do. in Near Do.	,,	1	,,
31	Do. in further Do.	1	2	14
32	Middle Finchams	14	3	20
33	Further Do.	15	,,	,,
34	Piece in Near Parsons Hole Furlong	1	3	12
35	Kinneys House Garden and Pightle	2	,,	12
36	Cottage and Garden	,,	,,	30

		A	R	P
Total		612	1	13

Parish of Syderstone

[*Left-hand page*] Coulsey Savory's Farm. [MAP XVI]

[a1. Plate LXXX]

Coulsey Savory
Tenant

16th a			A	R	P
	1	House Buildings Yard &c.	3	,,	12
	2	Shepherd's Pightle	7	,,	1
	3	Plantation	,,	1	6
	4	Do.	1	,,	19
	5	Do.	4	,,	20
	6	Do.	2	2	10
	7	Shepherd's House and Garden	,,	1	14
	8	Stack Brake	56	3	20
	9	Barn Brake	58	1	17
	10	Fakenham Road Brake	34	1	21
	11	Do.	27	3	,,
	12	Do. Do. 36 Acres	36	1	6
	13	Point Close Brake	35	,,	13
	14	Point Close	15	2	36
	15	Seventeen Acres	18	1	4
	16	Thirteen Acres	14	,,	4
	17	Horse Brake (exclusive of Glebe and			
		Marquis Townsend's Lands)	62	1	30
	18	Home Close exclusive of Glebe	40	3	10
	19	Brickiln Brake exclusive of Glebe	49	2	7
	20	Lodge Hill Brake exclusive of Glebe	39	2	10
	21	Three Furlong Brake exclusive of Glebe	62	2	3
	22	Bunting Path Close	20	2	15
	23	Rooks Close	16	,,	8

			A	R	P
24	Wells Forty Acres exclusive of Glebe		43	3	26
25	Wicker Close		14	2	13
26	Twenty seven Acres		26	2	15
27	Blacksmiths Close in 4 Parts		37	2	15
28	Warren Brake		16	2	24
29	Wicken Common		56	,,	12
30	Cottage and Garden		,,	,,	37
31	Garden		,,	2	32

[a32. Plate LXXXI]

		A	R	P
32	House and Garden	1	1	6
33	Orchard	3	1	7
34	Plantation	1	,,	18
35	Paddock	45	,,	6
36	Wells Road Piece	25	,,	33
37	Plantation	,,	,,	36
38	Bunting Path Brake exclusive of Glebe	84	3	22
39	Swimmers Brake exclusive of Glebe	63	1	14
40	Twenty Acres exclusive of Marquis Townsends	14	3	11
41	London Way	14	,,	32
42	Far Swimmers Meadow	6	,,	,,
43	Near Do.	11	1	,,
44	Hall Lane Close	4	3	17
45	Do.	6	3	18
46	The Cover	12	3	28

		A	R	P
	Total	1098	1	28

Parish of Syderstone

[*Left-hand page*] Nicholas Savory's Farm [MAP XVII]

[b1. Plate LXXXII]

Nicholas Savory
Tenant

			A	R	P
Map 17th b	1	House Building Yard &c.	2	2	15
	2	Backside	59	,,	23
	3	Stackyard	1	,,	8
	4	Blacksmith's Pightle	5	2	28
	5	Calves Pightle	6	0	37
	6	Pightle	1	2	29
	7	Coopers Brake	52	1	19

		A	R	P
8	Boarpit Brake	40	1	24
9	Dovehouse Yard exclusive of Glebe	36	2	21
10	Three cornered Piece	4	3	35
11	Manor Lings	25	3	30
12	Cover Brake	32	2	20
13	Burnham Brake exclusive of Glebe	39	1	15
14	Upper Blackhill	31	2	,,
15	Great Cover Close	64	2	18
16	Lower Blackhills	20	2	1
17	Creak Pasture Brake exclusive of Glebe	13	2	7
18	Cover seventeen Acres	18	2	2
19	First Cover Close exclusive of Glebe	21	1	22
20	Creak Pasture Forty Acres	42	1	1
21	Middle Cover Close	22	2	32
22	Further Do.	23	,,	8
23	Fifty two Acres	54	2	,,
24	Saffron Brake exclusive of Glebe	63	2	10
25	Bush Brake exclusive of Glebe	62	3	7
26	Path adjoining Wells Road Close	,,	3	33
27	Shoulder of Mutton exclusive of Glebe	64	,,	32
28	Cottage and Garden	,,	1	2

[b29. Plate LXXXIII]

		A	R	P
29	Cottage and Garden	,,	,,	16
30	Rooks Close	20	,,	,,
31	Daws Brake exclusive of Glebe	49	3	12
32	Cover Sixty Acres	64	1	8
33	Field Barn & Yard	,,	3	16
34	Hall Lane Brake exclusive of Glebe	21	2	32
35	Thirty Acres	33	3	37
36	Eighteen Acres	23	1	23
37	Marlpit Close	16	,,	34
38	Great Furze Cover Piece	29	1	38
39	Little Do. Do.	17	,,	28
40	Burnham Close	21	1	2
41	Rush Pit Brake	39	3	4
42	Great Common	147	,,	24

[b43. Plate LXXXIV]

		A	R	P
43	Cottage and Garden	,,	,,	36

[b44. Plate LXXXV]

		A	R	P
44	Cottage and Garden	,,	1	9

		A	R	P
Total		1331	2	38

MAPS and PLATES

56

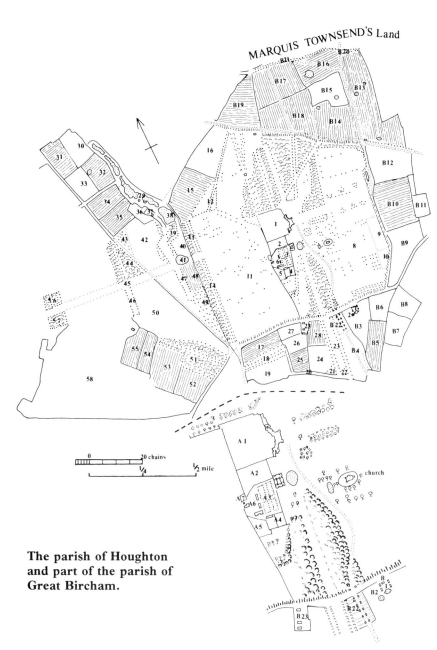

MARQUIS TOWNSEND'S Land

**The parish of Houghton
and part of the parish of
Great Bircham.**

MAP I. Letters A, B. Houghton. *Note: numerals without a letter-code should be
read as being prefixed by the letter-code A (e.g. 12 = A12).*

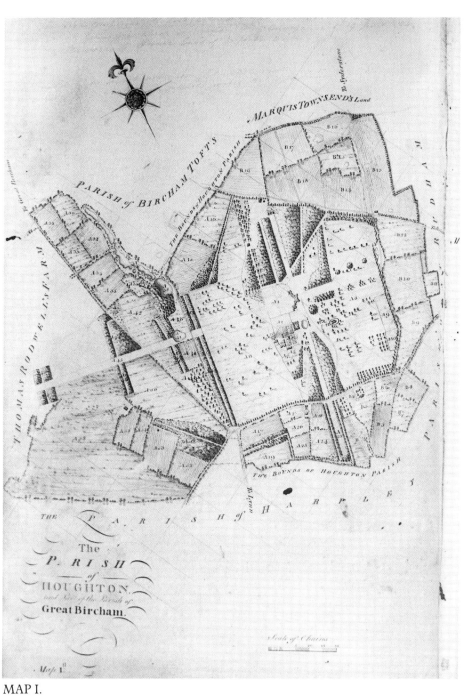

MAP I.

58

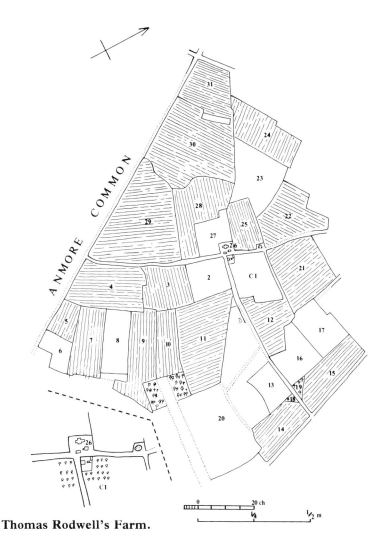

ANMORE COMMON

Thomas Rodwell's Farm.

0   20 ch
¼   ½ m

MAP II. Letter C. Great Bircham. *Note: all numerals on this map should be read as being prefixed by the letter-code C (e.g. 30 = C30).*

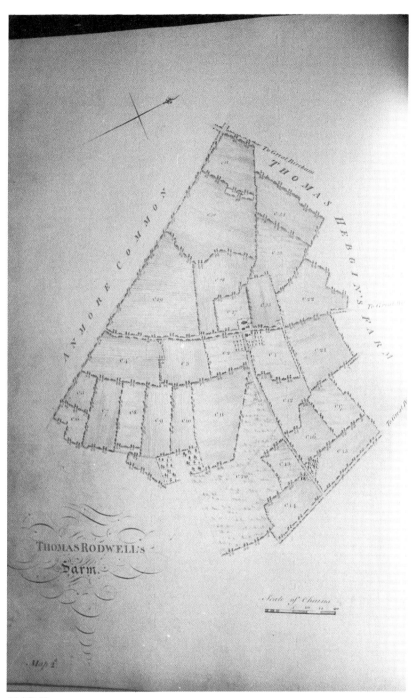

MAP II.

60

Edmund Holland's Farm.

MAP III. Letters D, E, F. Great Bircham. *Note: numerals without a letter-code should be read as being prefixed by the letter-code D (e.g. 22 = D22).*

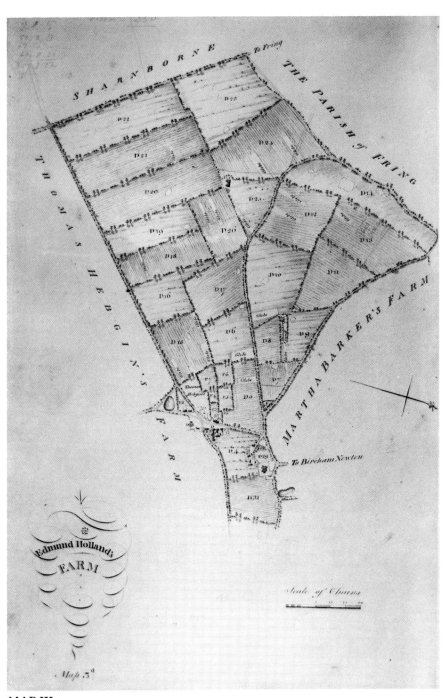

MAP III.

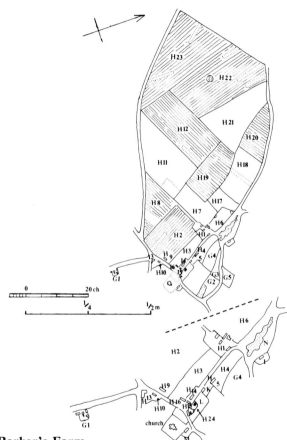

Martha Barker's Farm.

MAP IV. Letters G, H, I, K, L, M, N. Great Bircham.

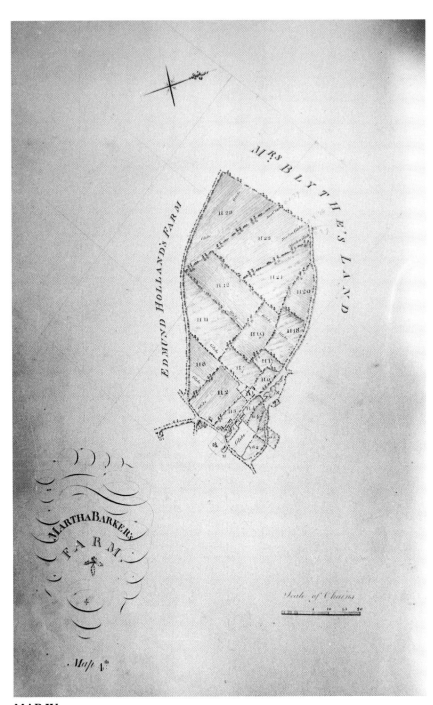

MAP IV.

64

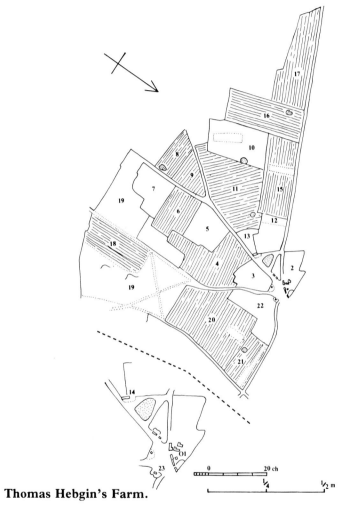

Thomas Hebgin's Farm.

MAP IVa. Letter O. Great Bircham. *Note: all numerals on this map should be read as being prefixed by the letter-code O (e.g. 5 = O5).*

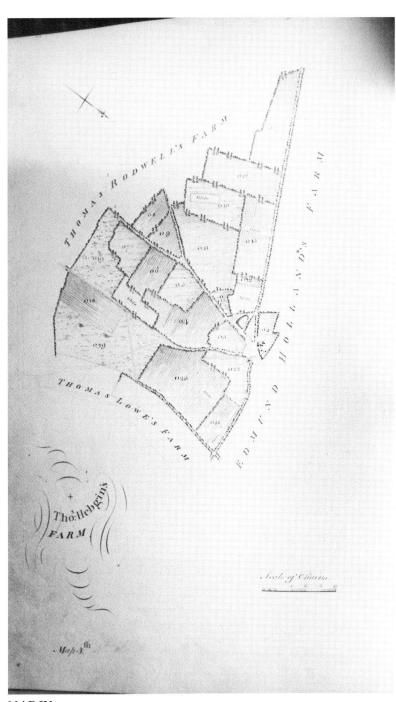

MAP IVa.

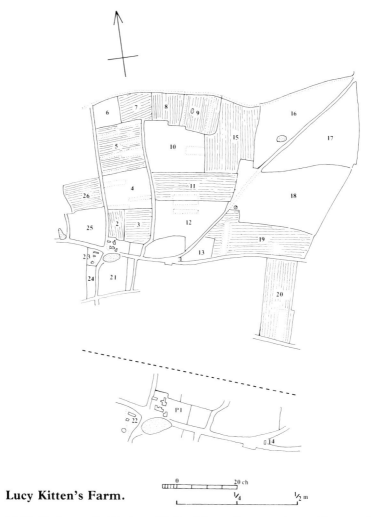

Lucy Kitten's Farm.

0   20 ch

¼   ½ m

MAP V. Letter P. Bircham Tofts. *Note: all numerals on this map should be read as being prefixed by the letter-code P (e.g. 15 = P15).*

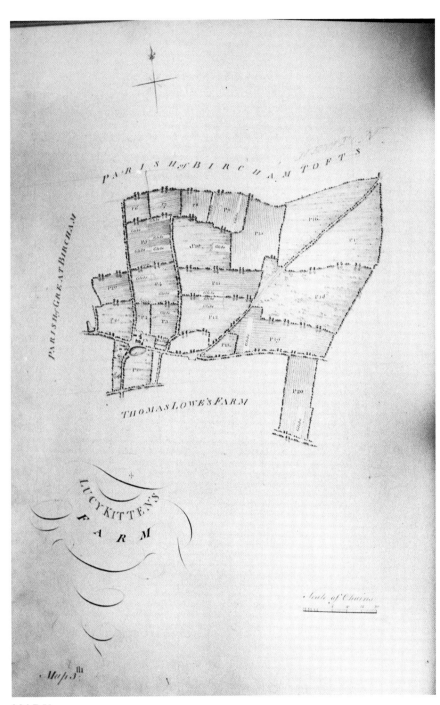

MAP V.

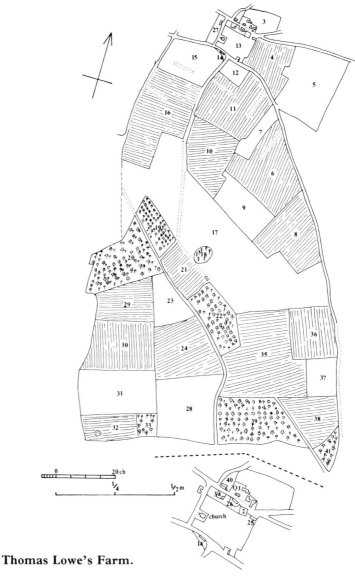

Thomas Lowe's Farm.

MAP VI. Letter Q. Bircham Tofts. *Note: all numerals on this map should be read as being prefixed by the letter-code Q (e.g. 24 = Q24).*

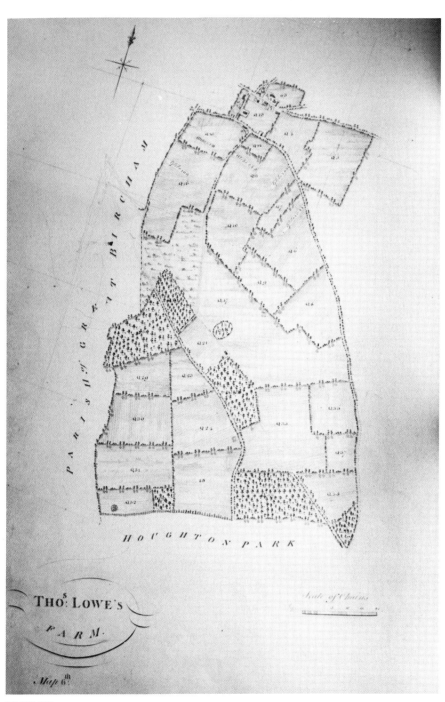

MAP VI.

Widow Blythe's Farm.

MAP VII. Letter R. Bircham Newton. *Note: all numerals on this map should be read as being prefixed by the letter-code R (e.g. 7 = R7).*

71

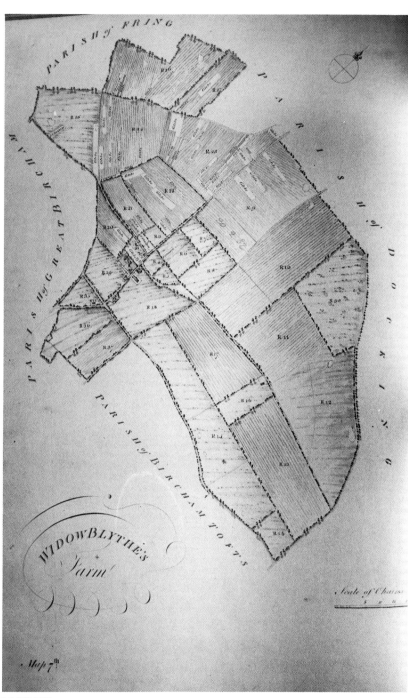

MAP VII.

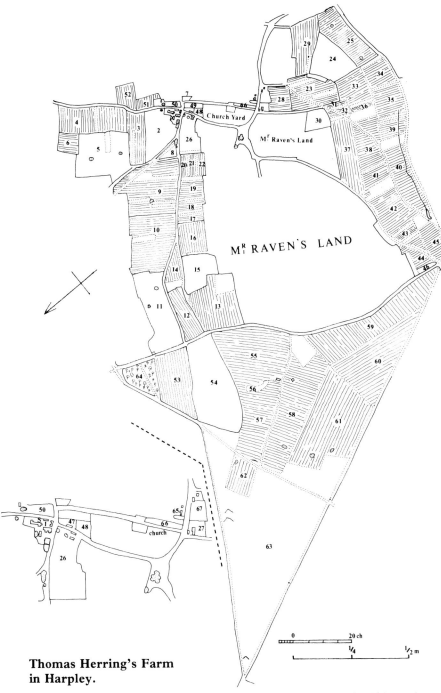

**Thomas Herring's Farm
in Harpley.**

MAP VIII. Letter S. Harpley. *Note: all numerals on this map should be read as
being prefixed by the letter-code S (e.g. 55 = S55).*

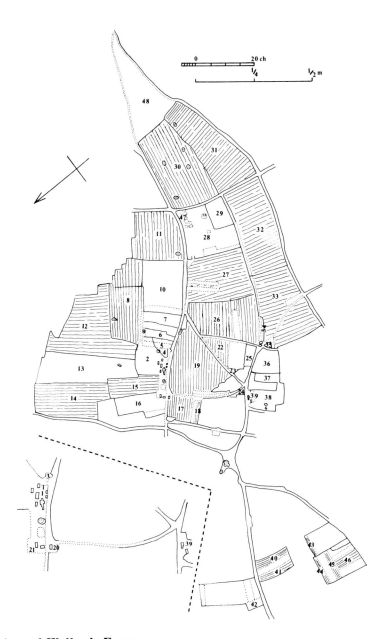

Edmund Walker's Farm.

MAP IX. Letter T. Harpley. *Note: all numerals on this map should be read as being prefixed by the letter-code T (e.g. 27 = T27).*

74

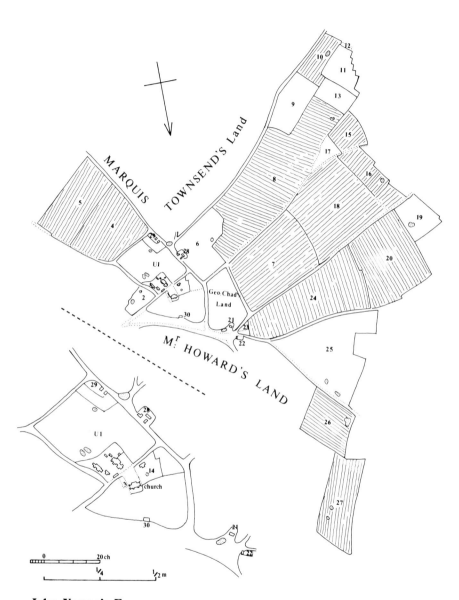

John Young's Farm.

MAP X. Letter U. West Rudham. *Note: all numerals on this map should be read as being prefixed by the letter-code U (e.g. 7 = U7).*

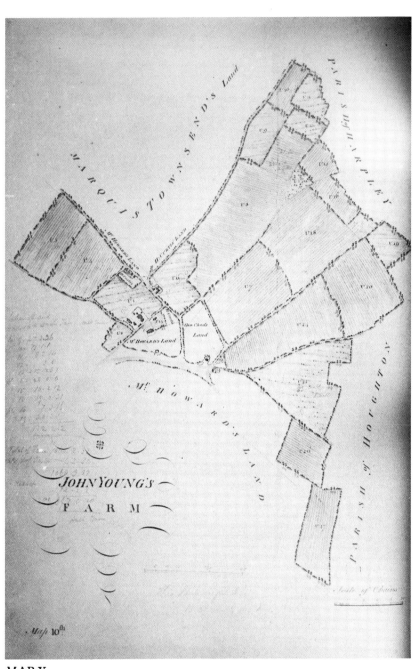

MAP X.

76

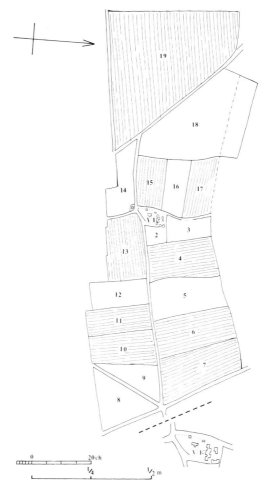

Ling House Farm.
Richard Stanton, Tenant.

MAP XI. Letter V. Dersingham. *Note: all numerals on this map should be read as being prefixed by the letter-code V (e.g. 12 = V12).*

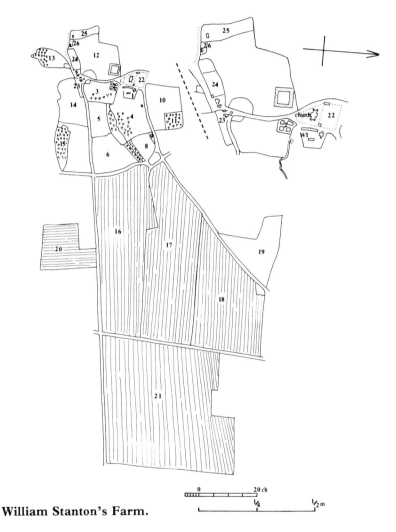

William Stanton's Farm.

MAP XII. Letter W. Dersingham. *Note: all numerals on this map should be read as being prefixed by the letter-code W (e.g. 16 = W16).*

Anthony Beck's Farm.

MAP XIII. Letter X. Great Massingham. *Note: all numerals on this map should be read as being prefixed by the letter-code X (e.g. 9 = X9).*

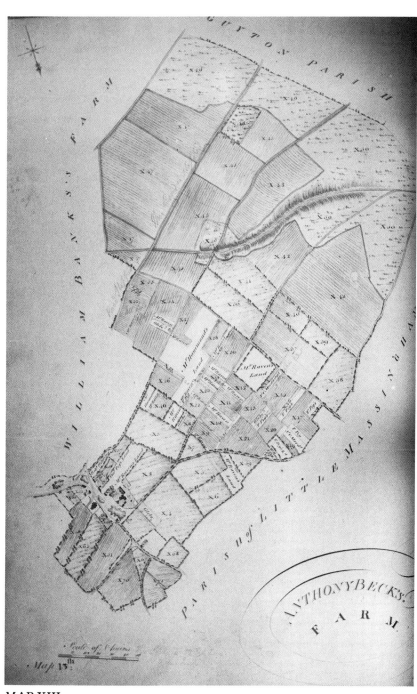

MAP XIII.

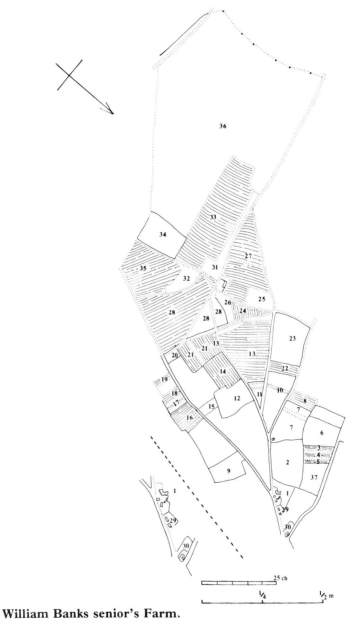

William Banks senior's Farm.

MAP XIV. Letter Y. Great Massingham. *Note: all numerals on this map should be read as being prefixed by the letter-code Y (e.g. 22 = Y22).*

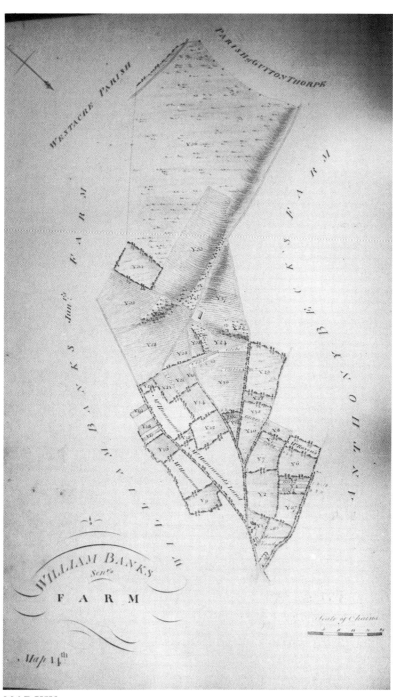

MAP XIV.

William Banks junior's Farm.

MAP XV. Letter Z. Great Massingham. *Note: all numerals on this map should be read as being prefixed by the letter-code Z (e.g. 4 = Z4).*

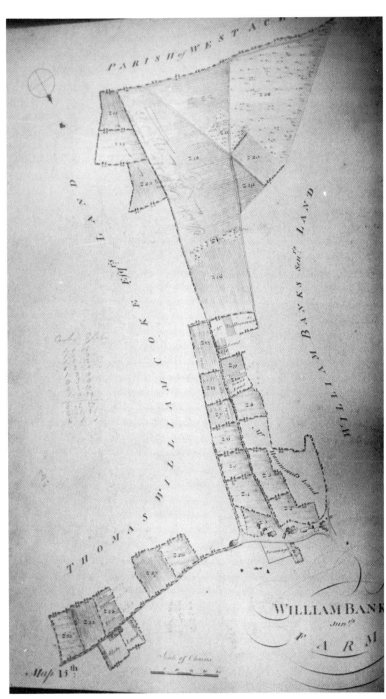

MAP XV.

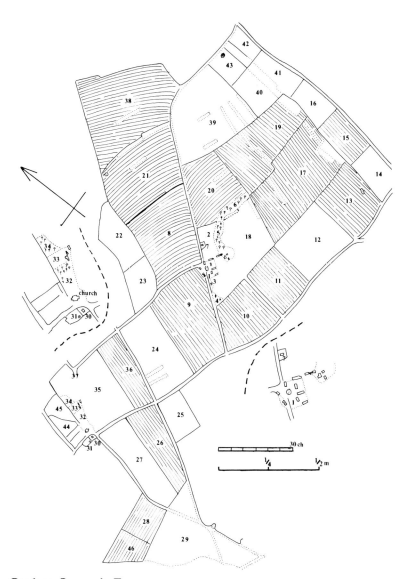

Coulsey Savory's Farm.

MAP XVI. Letter a. Syderstone. *Note: all numerals on this map should be read as being prefixed by the letter-code a (e.g. 5 = a5).*

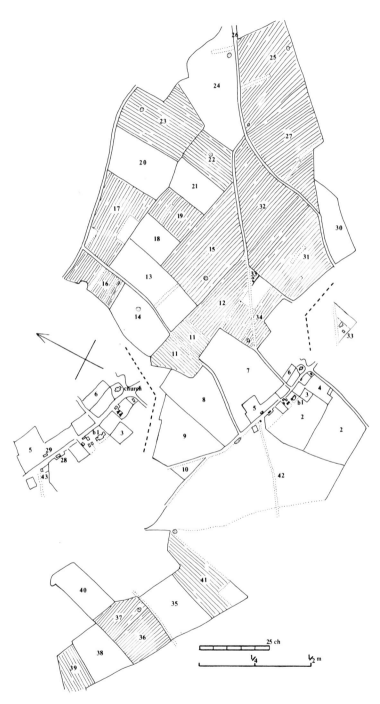

MAP XVII. Letter b. Syderstone. *Note: all numerals on this map should be read as being prefixed by the letter-code b (e.g. 13 = b13).*

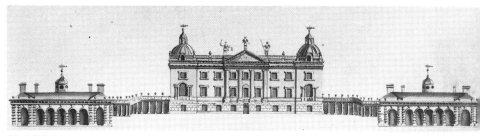

PLATE I. A1.

PLATE II. B1.

PLATE III. B22.

PLATE IV. B23.

PLATE V. C1.

PLATE VI. D1 D2 D3.

PLATE VII. D25.

PLATE VIII. D27.

PLATE IX. D28.

PLATE X. D30.

PLATE XI. E.

PLATE XII. F1.

PLATE XIII. F8.

PLATE XIV. G1.

PLATE XV. H1.

LATE XVI. H5.

PLATE XVII. H9.

PLATE XVIII. H13.

95

PLATE XIX. H14.

PLATE XX. H15.

PLATE XXI. H16.

PLATE XXII. I.

LATE XXIII. K.

LATE XXIV. L.

98

PLATE XXV. M.

PLATE XXVI. O1.

PLATE XXVII. O14.

PLATE XXVIII. O23.

PLATE XXIX. P1.

PLATE XXX. P14.

PLATE XXXI. P22.

PLATE XXXII. Q1.

PLATE XXXIII. Q14.

PLATE XXXIV. Q25.

PLATE XXXV. Q26

PLATE XXXVI. Q34.

PLATE XXXVII. Q40.

PLATE XXXVIII. R1.

PLATE XXXIX. R28.

PLATE XL. R29.

PLATE XLI. R31.

PLATE XLII. R32.

PLATE XLIII. R33.

PLATE XLIV. R34.

PLATE XLV. S1.

PLATE XLVI. S26.

PLATE XLVII. S27.

PLATE XLVIII. S47.

PLATE XLIX. S50.

PLATE L. S65.

PLATE LI. S67.

PLATE LII. T1.

112

PLATE LIII. T20.

PLATE LIV. T21.

PLATE LV. T39.

PLATE LVI. U1.

PLATE LVII. U14.

PLATE LVIII. U21.

PLATE LIX. U22.

*LATE LX. U28.

PLATE LXI. U29.

PLATE LXII. V1.

PLATE LXIII. W1.

PLATE LXIV. W23.

PLATE LXV. W24.

PLATE LXVI. W25.

PLATE LXVII. W26.

PLATE LXVIII. X1.

120

PLATE LXIX. X52.

PLATE LXX. X65.

PLATE LXXI. X61, X64.

PLATE LXXII. X53.

PLATE LXXIII. X55.

PLATE LXXIV. X56.

PLATE LXXV. X69.

PLATE LXXVI. X72.

124

PLATE LXXVII. Y1.

PLATE LXXVIII. Y30.

PLATE LXXIX. Z1.

PLATE LXXX. a1.

PLATE LXXXI. a32.

PLATE LXXXII. b1.

PLATE LXXXIII. b29.

LATE LXXXIV. b43.

PLATE LXXXV. b44.

APPENDICES

APPENDIX I
MAP OF PARISHES AND FARMS
INCLUDED IN SURVEY

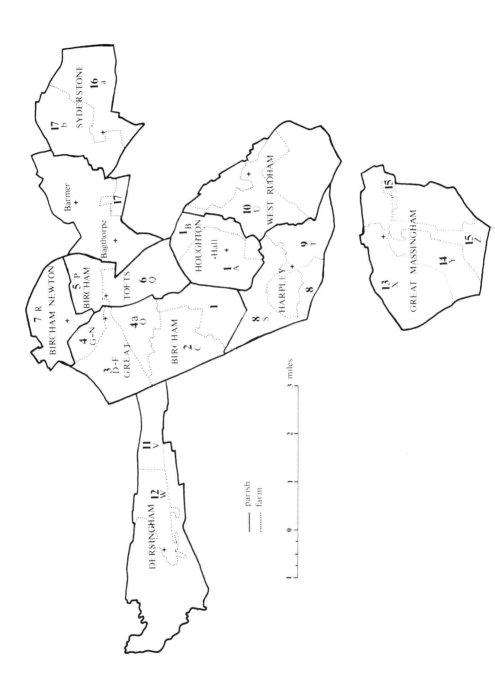

MAP I. HOUGHTON. Letters A and B.

For detailed comments on this map see above pp. 14-24.

In 1800 the Demesne Farm was run from the farmhouse at A.6. Much of the farm on Map I, including the 290 acres of the Old Common, is in the parish of Great Bircham. A.36 is the site of one of the major kilns producing bricks for the new house and its ancillary buildings, vast quantities being made there until at least 1744[99]. The Demesne Farm, excluding the park, comprises: *arable*, 229 acres — 21.7% of the farm; *pasture*, 571 acres — 54.2%; *wood*, 255 acres — 24.1%.

Mitchell's Farm was run from the Village Farm, B.1. On Map I it is arranged round the park in a series of large brecks and closes, the boundaries of some of which appear on the maps of 1720. Brickiln Breck (B.16) was there, in a slightly larger form, in 1720, and may still have been producing bricks in the 1730s.

Mitchell's farm comprises: *arable*, 355 acres — 66.8%; *pasture*, 168 acres — 31.7%; *wood*, 7 acres — 1.5%.

MAP II GREAT BIRCHAM. Letter C.

The manor of Great Bircham was bought by Col. Robert Walpole in 1688, after being surveyed in the previous year by 'Mr Hamond'.[100] A fine map had been made by John Madison between 1600 and 1609[101] and it may have been because of the existence of this map and survey that Thomas Badeslade did not survey Great Bircham in 1720. The parish was enclosed in 1740, when it was surveyed by John Thompson of Newcastle-upon-Tyne. The field-book of this survey is at Houghton,[102] but the map to which it refers does not appear to have survived there. The field-book, referring to the pre-enclosure situation, lists 13 farms. The largest is Heath Farm (538 acres); there are three of 200-300 acres, four of 100-200 acres, and the remaining five are under 100 acres. The enclosure brought a radical redistribution of land: Heath Farm rose to 877 acres, four others were between 288 and 410 acres, and there were six more of under 100 acres each, two of them under 10 acres. The commons, lanes, and wastes dropped from 1103 to 936 acres.

There was obviously a great deal of change in the landscape between 1600 and 1800. In 1600 the site of Heath Farm was empty; the road approaching the house from the east in 1800 continued along the long boundary from C.26 to C.31, and the road by the north-east of C.21 continued through C.12 to the Heath, C.20, and thence to Harpley Common. The road running by C.15 and C.14 did not exist in 1600, when C.3, C.11, C.20, C.28, and C.29 were open heath. The long straight road on the left of Map II is the Peddars Way, a Roman road, and was obviously there in 1600. The fields C.13 and C.14 were there in 1600, as was the crooked boundary between C.3 and C.4 and C.9 and C.10. The other fields on Map II bear little or no relation to what was there in 1600. The two unnumbered, wooded enclosures are part of the West View of Houghton Park.

Rodwell's Farm: *arable* 647 acres — 72.3%; *pasture* 244 acres — 27.3%.

MAP III. GREAT BIRCHAM. Letters D, E, F.

The area in which the enclosure of F.8 stands, and the open area between F.1 and D.1, 2, 3 is virtually the same as on the map of 1600, where it was called Upgate Green; the encroachment F.8 was then divided into east-west strips of varying length, each with a cottage at the east end fronting the road. The pit was virtually the same shape and size. In 1600, as in 1800, Upgate Green was fringed with houses (see notes on houses on Maps III, IV and IVa). The road pattern west of the church in 1600 was very much the same as in 1800 and the present day. In 1600 the looping road westwards from the south-west corner of the churchyard was called Hungate, and was connected with the road going east from Upgate Green by a zigzagging hedged road. The area west of the churchyard in 1600 was divided into six hedged enclosures of various shapes and sizes, and contained five houses — one next to the rectory, three fronting Hungate, and one at the western tip (see notes on D.28, D.30 and H.13). It was obviously an early enclosure of an open green. Middle Saxon pottery and a Saxo-Norman pottery kiln have been found on the site.[103] In 1600 there were four more houses on the south side of Hungate (see note on D.27).

[99]CUL, Cholm. 23/2.
[100]CUL, Cholm. 15/1.
[101]Houghton, Maps 6 and 7.
[102]Houghton, M.11.d.
[103]*East Anglian Archaeology*, viii. 33-43.

Around the central area of the village in 1600 were a large number of small hedged enclosures, most of them long and narrow, suggesting enclosure from strips or holdings in the open fields.

The road at the top of Map III is the Peddars Way. The road joining it from F.8 was not straight in 1600. At that date a fieldroad ran from F.2 in a shallow curve to the crossroads on the Peddars Way, which was also the starting point for another road, Docking Gate Way, that ran past the field-barn site and continued as the west boundary of D.25. The track from the field-barn to the Peddars Way on Map III was not there in 1600. The other roads on Map III were the same in 1600, when the whole of this area was a mass of strips and furlongs, the only enclosures being adjacent to the farmhouses. None of the pits on Map III are shown on the map of 1600.

Some rearrangement and amalgamation of farmland took place between 1740 and 1753, for the fieldbook of that year[104] has no single farm comparable in size to Holland's.

Holland's farm: *arable* 494 acres — 56.8%; *pasture* 374 acres — 43.2%.

MAP IV. GREAT BIRCHAM. Letters G, H, I, K, L, M, N.

In 1600 the road skirting H.18 and H.20 was a wide droveway, bending round along the straight north edge of Map IV to join the Fryng Waye at the top of the map. The direction of the open-field strips is shown by the dotted lines of the glebe, and in 1600 the whole area was a mass of strips and furlongs. The large pit in H.22 was not shown in 1600, but one of a similar size lay a little to the east near the south end of the longest glebe strip in Map IV and was called Dudlo pitt. This is represented on the modern O.S. map by a longish depression. In 1600 a solid hedgeline ran along most of the line from H.7 to H.20, and may have represented the earliest western boundary of the moor; H.17, H.18 and the eastern part of H.7 were small hedged enclosures. In 1600 the north part of Map IV was called Nethergate Moor, but the long irregular pit was not shown. The road from the moor to Bircham Tofts, passing between G.3 and G.5, was there in 1600, but had disappeared by 1838; the rounded area it encloses was no doubt a medieval encroachment on Nethergate Moor, and the large pit that takes up much of G.2 is shown on the map of 1600.

Martha Barker's farm: *arable*, 161 acres — 64.9%; *pasture*, 87 acres — 35.1%.

Robert Sparrow's farm: *pasture*, 9 acres.

MAP IVa. GREAT BIRCHAM. Letter O.

In the written survey Thomas Hebgin's farm is referred to 'Map 4th', which is a mistake, as the previous map is Map 4. The map of Hebgin's farm is numbered 5, which is also wrong, as the next map, of Lucy Kitten's farm, is also numbered 5. Hebgin's farm and its map, therefore, is here referred to as IVa.

Hebgin's farm fills the area between maps II and III. The northern boundary is the road from Upgate Green (see notes on Map II), and the forked road going south-west leads to the former heath. O.19 is heath, and two of the three existing tumuli there are shown. Neither the road crossing O.18 nor the road leaving it north-east across O.19 are shown on the map of 1600. On that map the other road crossing O.19 is called Rudham Way, and from the same starting point at the funnel-shaped northern corner of O.19 another road ran past the tumuli (which are not shown on the map of 1600). From the same corner of O.19 yet another road ran across O.4 to Upgate Green. In 1600 the area was moderately stripped, and many of the field boundaries of 1800 follow the furlong bounds of 1600. None of the pits on Map IVa except the large one at Upgate Green appears on the map of 1600.

Hebgin's farm: *arable*, 310 acres — 74.4%; *pasture*, 101 acres — 24.6%.

MAP V. BIRCHAM TOFTS. Letter P.

The manor of Bircham Tofts was bought by Walpole *c.*1705. Badeslade's map of 1720 shows some stripped furlongs at P.4 and P.5, but most of the area was even then in great closes and brakes. A fieldbook, based on the 1720 survey but 'rectified' in 1753,[105] shows this farm, in the tenancy of Mr Humphrey, to consist of 105 acres of brake, 100 acres of inclosure, 168 acres of infield, and 77 acres of sheep-walk on the common. There had been a considerable consolidation of small fields and strips since 1720. The road pattern of 1720 is largely unchanged on Map V and at the present day, except that the field road forming the northern boundary has virtually gone. The legend here should read 'Parish of Bircham Newton'. P.18 is common on Map V, and

[104]Houghton, M.24.g.
[105]Houghton, M.7.b and Maps 10 and 11.

P.16 and P.17 were also probably common before the late-sixteenth century. The large pond opposite P.1 is still there, but the pits in P.9, P.16, and P.18 no longer exist.

Lucy Kitten's farm: *arable*, 191 acres — 41.2%; *pasture*, 273 acres — 58.8%.

MAP VI. BIRCHAM TOFTS. Letter Q.

The map of 1720[106] presents a very similar pattern of roads and fields to that on Map VI. The fields are large, with very little stripping. Mr Brown's farm in 1753 comprised 339 acres of breck, 42 acres of inclosure, 168 acres of infield, and 107 acres of common sheepwalk. Nurseries, i.e. plantations, and lands not let to farm totalled another 353 acres.[107] Q.17 is called Blackground Common in the survey. 'Blackground' often has some reference to a Roman site, and the 'tower' on Bircham Common, which is not shown on Map VI but lies in the angle between the diagonal road in Q.17 and the south-west side of Q.10, is thought by some to be Roman.[108]

Lowe's Farm: *arable*, 458 acres — 47.7%; *pasture*, 388 acres — 40.4; *wood*, 115 acres — 11.9% (see note on Map I).

MAP VII. BIRCHAM NEWTON. Letter R.

The manor of Bircham Newton came into the possession of the Robsarts in 1496-7. In 1588, on the death of the Earl of Leicester, who had married Amy Robsart, it came into the hands of Calybut Walpole, whose grandfather Edward had married Lucy Robsart. The manor extended into the parish of Great Bircham. On Badeslade's map of 1720[109] all the land west of the road-line R.37 to R.9 and R.10 lies in 22 furlongs, all heavily stripped. East of the road are 20 furlongs, unstripped. This latter was undoubtedly the brake and common area. R.30, the common, is roughly in the position of the common of 1720, but the other field divisions of Map VII do not follow the furlong boundaries of the earlier map, and very few of the boundaries of the western half of the parish are the same at the two dates. The road pattern, on the other hand, changed little between 1720 and 1800, except for the removal of 'Burnham Way alias Stanhoe Way' that ran diagonally north-east across R.15, R.16, and R.13, and the addition of a field road at the north side of R.22. The field book of 1753 shows less consolidation of small holdings than at Bircham Tofts, but by that date the several small farms of 1720 had been reduced to two large farms: William Young's (875 acres) and Charles Young's (120 acres), with 49 acres of glebe and three very small owners.[110] William Young was at R.1, and Charles Young at R.29.

The north-east quarter of Map VII has been obliterated by the airfield, and the Construction Industry Training Centre occupies much of R.13 and R.14. Otherwise the road and field pattern is much as it was in 1800, although some of the roads are now field tracks or paths. Henry Blyth of Bircham Newton died in 1784.

Widow Blythe's Farm: *arable*, 647 acres — 57.7%; *pasture*, 474 acres — 42.3%.

MAP VIII. HARPLEY. Letter S.

The manor of Houghton, which the Walpoles had held since the 13th century, had appurtenances in Harpley, and in 1324-5 Sir Henry de Walpole had tenements held of the manor of Uphall there. This manor was united to Gourney's manor in the 14th century.[111] In about 1642 Sir William Yelverton sold the united manors to John Walpole of Brunsthorpe, brother of Robert Walpole of Houghton, and on the death of John's heir, his daughter Elizabeth Pepys, in 1668, the estate passed to his nephew Sir Edward Walpole of Houghton. The manor of Bircham Tofts also had appurtenances in Harpley.

Badeslade's map of 1720[112] shows many of the fields south-east of the road across the centre of Map VIII (Harpley Dams to Bircham) heavily stripped. North-west of the road there are large brakes of similar size and shape to those of 1800. S.54 was wooded in 1720. The road pattern changed very little between the two dates, although two footpaths were closed in 1789.[113] The modern by-pass runs north of the village, but otherwise the modern road-pattern is very much the same as in 1800, with a few closures. Gone is the road from Houghton across the south-east end of the common, the road on the north-west of S.64, the road skirting S.13 and S.15 (this had gone by 1824), and the field road beginning between S.23 and S.28. The road from Harpley to New Houghton, bordering S.8 and S.9, was replaced by the straight road soon

[106]Houghton, Maps 10 and 11.
[107]Houghton, M.7.b.
[108]Broome, *Houghton*, p.19.
[109]Houghton, Maps 8 and 9.
[110]Ibid. and M.6.d, M.7.h.
[111]F. Blomefield, *History of Norfolk* (2nd ed.), viii. 453.
[112]Houghton, Map 24.
[113]NRO, C/Sce 1/3. 296.

after 1800. The Common, S.63, has three of the existing tumuli marked, and all the fields west of the Houghton-Harpley Dams road are 'brakes', a name indicating their heathy sheep-walk origin — the road from Harpley to this area is 'shipgate'. Very few of the numerous pits on the modern map appear on Map VIII. The map shows the northern part only of the settlement. The churchyard is the empty rectangle opposite the north end of S.66.

Herring's farm was large and included all the north-west part of this large and strangely-shaped parish. The Peddars Way, the long straight road on the right-hand side of the bottom half of Map VIII, forms that part of the parish boundary, and the road leaving it at an acute angle at the bottom and going to S.64 is also a boundary.

Herring's Farm: *arable*, 680 acres — 65.9%; *pasture*, 352 acres — 34.1%.

MAP IX. HARPLEY. Letter T.
On the map of 1720[114] most of the furlongs north of the hedgeline between T.10/11 and T.27/28 are heavily stripped, although there are also some medium-sized closes taken in from the strips of the open field, particularly on either side of the road past T.1. South of that line are large brakes similar to those on Map VIII. The 'Old mill' stands within the dotted key-shaped plot in T.28. The road pattern of 1720 did not change much before 1800, except for the loss of a track, called in 1720 Peddars Way, that ran due north from the south-west corner of T.25 to the northern corner of T.17. Its line can be seen on Map IX on the wavy boundary of T.19, although the track itself is reasonably straight on Badeslade's map. Map IX shows most of the south-east part of the parish. The nineteenth century saw little alteration to the road pattern of 1800, the greatest loss being the field-road from T.24 to T.20, which does not appear on the tithe map of 1838. T.48, now Harpley Common, is 'sheepwalk' in 1800, and it seems quite likely that the common formerly extended at least as far as T.47, and probably went as far as the hedgeline mentioned above.

Walker's Farm: *arable*, 450 acres — 72.2%; *pasture*, 173 acres — 27.8%.

MAP X. WEST RUDHAM. Letter U.
According to Blomefield and Bryant, all three medieval manors in West Rudham — Ferrers, Castle Acre Priory, and Northall or St. Faith's — had come into the hands of the Townshends of Raynham by about the middle of the seventeenth century.[115] Syderstone manor had appurtenances amounting to a berewick in West Rudham, and it may be these that formed the core of Young's farm, but it should be noted that U.4 and U.5 are called 'St Faize' in the survey, and the fact that there are manorial records of both Ferrers and Northall in the Houghton archives suggests that some exchange and rearrangement took place. Sir Robert Walpole was negotiating to buy Lady Seaman's Rudham estate in 1721.[116] Both the road and field pattern of Map 10 survive in the modern landscape, although — rather surprisingly — some of the larger fields (e.g. U.8 and U.24), were subdivided in the nineteenth century. Washpit Drove, which now runs south across the east end of U.8, is not shown on Map X but was in use in 1824, and U.1 is now bisected by one of the headwaters of the River Wensum that starts from the pit between U.28 and U.29.

Young's Farm: *arable*, 756 acres — 72.9%; *pasture*, 280 acres — 27.1%.

In 1842 the tithe map shows another Cholmondeley farm of 295 acres, mainly in the north of the parish, with the farmhouse at The Grove and occupied by Robert Algar, while 151 acres between the Massingham and Harpley roads is farmed by William Herring of Norwich, who also had land in Harpley. Hall Farm, occupied by Thomas Tingey, is only 888 acres.

MAP XI. LING HOUSE FARM, DERSINGHAM. Letter V.
Fragments of a map of 1693 of Ling House Farm made for Robert Britiffe cover only the western half of Map XI.[117] Large unstripped fields — North, Barley, Wheat, and South Furlongs — run east-west, and V.2, V.3, and the western part of V.13 lie in five closes called North, Barne, Claypit, Turkey, and South Closes. The total acreage of the farm in 1693 was 292 acres in enclosures, $174\frac{1}{2}$ acres in open field, and $18\frac{1}{4}$ acres in Shernborne Field. Britiffe (1661/2-1749) was a lawyer employed by the Walpoles, and may well have been acting for Robert Walpole the elder. Blomefield says that Valentine Pell, being without issue, gave the manors of Shouldham Priory and Brooke Hall or Old Hall, in Dersingham, to Robert Walpole

[114]Houghton, Map 24.
[115]F. Blomefield, *History of Norfolk* (2nd ed.), vii. 158 sqq; T. H. Bryant, *Churches of Norfolk: Gallow*, pp. 114-5.
[116]J. H. Plumb, *Sir Robert Walpole*, i (1956) 361.
[117]Houghton, Map 13.

in 1685, while Plumb states that in 1697 Robert Walpole the elder bought his cousin Pell's estate at Dersingham and West Winch, worth £450 a year but burdened with two considerable life interests.[118] Ling House Farm — a name suggesting colonisation of heathland — probably consists largely of the lands of Shouldham Priory manor. The road at the bottom of Map XI is the Peddars Way, nearly $3\frac{1}{2}$ miles from Dersingham village. Hillington, Flitcham, Shernbourne, Snettisham, Great Bircham, and Harpley all reach up to the downland of the old Roman road in this way. There is a marlpit in the corner of V.14, and the claypit east of the house is marked on the map of 1693 but not on Map XI. The modern road and field pattern is very like that of 1800.

Stanton's Farm: *arable*, 345 acres — 62.1%; *pasture*, 210 acres — 37.9%.

MAP XII. DERSINGHAM. Letter W.

The manor of Brooke Hall or Old Hall passed, as described under Map XI, from the Pell family to the Walpoles towards the end of the seventeenth century. A map of the manors of Brooke Hall and Shouldham, undated but probably of 1720, is in pieces and incomplete.[119] Unfortunately it does not show the manor-house area, but the fields are still heavily stripped. On the map of 1800 the old moated site of the manor is in W.12 and is shown as a square; but the tithe map of 1839 has the north-east corner doubled inwards, a shape that approximates to that on modern maps and on the ground. In 1985 the moat was still there, and immediately south of it were the remains of a fine set of fishponds. An account book of the elder Robert Walpole has an entry for 1 September 1683: 'given att my cousen Valentine Pells when I had the carpe there 9s. 6d.'[120] W.2 is the walled garden which will be described under W.1. Most of the village of Dersingham stood at this time to the south and south-west of the moated site, strung along the looping road that edged Dersingham Common and Sandringham Warren.

Stanton's Farm: *arable*, 518 acres — 76.2%; *pasture*, 148 acres — 21.9%; *wood*, 12 acres — 1.8%.

MAP XIII. GREAT MASSINGHAM. Letter X.

The village of Great Massingham lies around an L-shaped green containing several large ponds. Massingham Priory, which stood on X.1 and X.2, was founded before 1260 as a hospital. It was not well endowed, and although the buildings were enlarged in 1302 it never became important, and in 1475 it became a cell of West Acre Priory. After the Dissolution it joined the capital manor, Dartfords, which had belonged to Dartford Nunnery since 1384, in the hands of Sir Thomas Gresham. Afterwards they came into the ownership of the Barkhams of South Acre, relatives by marriage of the Walpoles, and after passing briefly into the possession of the Yallops the manors were conveyed to Sir Robert Walpole.[121] After passing to the Duke of Norfolk at the Dissolution, Monks or Castle Acre Priory manor came to John Walpole of Harpley; after the death of his son William in 1587-8 it came into the hands of the Cokes, who also held the fourth manor, Felthams. Thomas Badeslade surveyed Great Massingham for Sir Robert Walpole, and his map is dated 1730.[122] East of the Peddars Way — the road on Map XIII across the centre from X.18/38 to X.35/45 — the fields of 1730 lay in a complicated pattern of small furlongs, partly in strips but with some amalgamations and unstripped closes. Some of the boundaries of these furlongs and closes are still traceable on Map XIII. Near the village the closes were less divided, but few boundaries here reappear on Map XIII. West of the Peddars Way were very large brakes, some corresponding with the boundaries on Map XIII. The road pattern scarcely changed between 1730 and 1800. The survey records the names of the former open fields — Hartswood, Greenway, Greyton or Guyton, Lynn etc. — which oddly do not occur as such on the map of 1730. Abbey Farm ran to the western boundary of the parish on Massingham Heath in 1800 and was bisected by the Peddars Way. The road pattern in 1985 is almost the same as in 1800, but the road between X.45 and X.47 has gone.

Beck's Farm: *arable*, 667 acres — 56.4%; *pasture*, 516 acres — 43.6%.

MAP XIV. GREAT MASSINGHAM. Letter Y.

In 1730 most of the southern half of Map XIV was large brakes and common, with the boundaries and road patterns much as in 1800. North of the road, now gone, from Y.20 to the five-way junction at Y.25 there were many small unstripped closes and amalgamated strips. On Map XIV William Banks' farm runs south-west from the village to the parish boundary on Mass-

[118]F. Blomefield, *History of Norfolk* (2nd ed.), viii. 394 sqq.; J. H. Plumb, *Men and Places*, 1963, p. 131.
[119]Houghton, Map 12.
[120]CUL, Cholm. 15/1.
[121]F. Blomefield, *History of Norfolk* (2nd ed.), ix. 4, 8.
[122]Houghton, Maps 14, 15.

136

ingham Heath. The Peddars Way runs diagonally across the centre of the farm from the south-west corner of Y.23 to Y.35, bending slightly to avoid the barn at Y.27, now Betts' Field Barn. Several roads marked on Map XIV went out of use in the nineteenth century: the road to the heath beginning near the north-east corner of Y.7; the road from Y.20 to the five-way junction with the Peddars Way; the road from the fork at Y.11 to the south-west corner of Y.28; and the road acting as the southern boundary of Y.28. The road from West Acre to Betts' Field Barn is not marked on Map XIV, although it appears on Faden's map of 1797 and the early editions of the ordnance survey maps. The brick kiln implied in Y.28 is located by the map of 1730 at the extreme north-eastern corner of the field opposite Y.20; to the south-east of the brick kiln and on the other side of the road to Castle Acre the 1730 map shows a lime kiln. Large quantities of bricks were brought from Massingham to Houghton from 1733 to 1744; the brickmaker was Edward Youngs.[123]

Banks' Farm: *arable*, 208 acres — 32.3%; *pasture*, 435 acres — 67.7%.

MAP XV. GREAT MASSINGHAM. Letter Z.

On the map of 1730 the fields Z.2 to Z.15 are part of a series of stripped furlongs, while the large southern brakes are much as they appear on the map of 1800. Most of the fields Z.26 to Z.33 were already enclosed in 1730. The road east of Z.4-6 is not shown on the 1730 map, but another road runs on the diagonal boundary between Z.1 and Z.4 and eventually joins the road to Rougham, which itself was simplified and straightened later in the eighteenth century. At the south end of Map XV is the road from Litcham to King's Lynn, which was then a main way from north and north-central Norfolk to the Wash but subsequently fell partly into disuse. The road on Map XV beginning between Z.19 and Z.20 and joining the main way is the Peddars Way, and the axis of the farm is the road from Massingham to Castle Acre. The tithe map of 1838 has no pond in the fattest section of the green and the west end of the green has more buildings than are shown on Map XV.

William Banks junior's Farm: *arable*, 317 acres — 48.6%; *pasture*, 345 acres — 51.4%.

MAP XVI. SYDERSTONE. Letter a.

Syderstone came to the possession of the Walpoles in 1588, when Calybut Walpole inherited it in the right of Lucy Robsart, his grandmother. Maps XVI and XVII cover practically the whole of the parish. Badeslade's map of 1720[124] shows that White Hall, a.1, had not then been built, and that most of the north and east of the parish consisted of a large number of moderately-stripped furlongs, of which the pieces of glebe on Map XVI are the remnants. A road that in 1720 ran in a curve from the south-west corner of a.24 to the north-east corner of a.9 has been replaced by 1800 by the straight road between a.9 and a.10, but from the neighbourhood of a.1 it runs to the boundary on Map XVI as in 1720. The road running west from a.1 was in 1720 a headland access to the furlongs. The field pattern was reconstructed between 1720 and 1800 to give larger, more regular fields, and only in part used the furlong boundaries. Two brakes in the area of a.10-12 were known in 1720 as Dead Mans Grave Breck; this lay on the parish boundary and could commemorate a suicide's grave,[125] or even a prehistoric barrow site. The Savory family farmed in Syderstone from at least the early seventeenth century, and continued there until 1851. The farms were sold by the Cholmondeley estate in 1920.

Coulsey Savory's Farm: *arable*, 611 acres — 56.1%; *pasture*, 469 acres — 43.1%; *wood*, 9 acres — 0.8%.

MAP XVII. SYDERSTONE. Letter b.

The map of 1720[126] shows a line of large closes north of the village street covering the southern halves of b.7-9. North of these closes are the furlongs of the open field, moderately stripped. The Common is in b.11, and The Cover occupies b.12, b.15, and a small part of b.32. Faden's map of 1797 shows the shape and disposition of both the common and the cover somewhat differently from Map XVII. In 1720 Syderstone Warren was the name given to b.42, and Lord Townsend's Warren lay over the parish boundary. Six tenements are shown north of the village street, and eleven to the south. The road pattern was slightly simplified between 1720 and 1800. The fields b.35-41 are in the parish of Bagthorpe.

Savory's Farm: *arable*, 760 acres — 54.1%; *pasture*, 645 acres — 45.9%.

[123]CUL, Cholm. 23/2.
[124]Houghton, Map 16.
[125]cf. Deadmans Grave on the Paston-Edingthorpe boundary, and Pigg's Grave at the junction of Briningham, Melton Constable, and Swanton Novers.
[126]Houghton, Map 16.

PLATE I. A.1. HOUGHTON HALL. *Total length 10¾". Viewed from the west.*
Some of the complicated history of the building of Houghton Hall has been discussed above, and this is not the place to go into it in depth. The house was completed in 1735, and has had relatively few alterations since. As built, there was a double staircase approaching the central door on the first or main floor on both the west and the east fronts. They were both decaying in 1773 and were taken down about 1780. In 1973 the staircase on the west front was rebuilt to the original design. The south wing, on the right of A.1, contained the kitchen, domestic offices, and some lodging rooms. According to Robinson, the north wing contained 'the brew-house and the wash-house, &c., and a very magnificent hall for a chapel, and a large room which looks on the parterre, designed for a gallery, there being the same in the opposite wing for a greenhouse'.[79] This suggests that a room in the south wing was the greenhouse; but Horace Walpole asserted that the greenhouse was in the north wing and was only converted to a gallery in 1743, after Sir Robert had brought to Houghton all the pictures from his house in Downing Street. The ceiling was said to be a copy of that in the inner library of St. Mark's in Venice, the design being brought back by Horace from his grand tour in 1739-41.[80] It looks as if Robinson got the two wings confused. The north wing was gutted by fire late in the eighteenth century, and partly rebuilt by the fourth Earl of Cholmondeley.[81] Hill's drawing shows nothing of the damage caused by the fire. Apart from the staircase, the Hall in A.1 is much the same as in 1985.

PLATE II B.1. JOHN MITCHELL, TENANT. *Village Farm. Oval 5½" x 3¾". Viewed from the north-north-west.*
On the map of 1720 the site of this farmhouse is Sallow Close Furlong. The farmstead does not appear on the map of 1723-9 but it is shown on all the maps of the 1730s, and was presumably part of the building programme of the few years after 1729. Plans at Houghton, undated but certainly of this period, give its ground-plan: parlour to the left of the door, measuring 21 by 17 feet; a small entrance-hall containing a dog-leg stair, with a small room behind it on the south side; kitchen, 21 by 17 feet, on the right of the entrance door. The left-hand bay of the lower range is a yard with a back door. Next right is a large backhouse, 20 by 18 feet, with backstairs, bread oven, and copper, and the room farthest right is the dairy. South of the house the plans show a ten-bay barn, 129 feet long, with two doors towards the ends on either side and lean-tos, probably animal houses, between the doors. A five-bay cartshed, with an attic and two dormers, stands on one side of the yard, and on the other is a two-room building with attic.[82] Map I shows the same buildings were still there in 1800. On B.1 the main door is of rail and panel construction, and has a rectangular fanlight over it. The dairy on the right, and the room over it, have slatted windows. The window over the secondary door has a curious diagonal across it. The waterbutt to the right of this door is the only one occurring in the survey. The present house is basically the same as that of 1800, but the roof is of blue pantiles and the three flat-roofed dormers have gone. Both ranges have dentellated cornices, and the main windows are now all sashes instead of the casements of 1800. A square two-storey block covers the secondary door. The barn survives.

PLATE III. B.22. HOUGHTON VILLAGE. *Width at bottom of drawing 6½". Viewed from the north.*
The foundations for the first houses in the new village were begun on 4th July 1729, and on 12th January following the painters began priming doors and windows.[83] The site chosen for the new village was a furlong of the old fields near the junction of two old roads from Houghton to Harpley. The cottages on B.22 are double cottages with a central stack and double-hipped roofs, and all but two on the left have a two-storey lean-to end-range added to the original building. On the drawing the pairs appear to be connected by high walls, which do not survive. The nearest house at the right-hand side has a small building nestling behind the curve of the wall, and there is an extra upstairs window in the main building. Hill found the perspective of the hips and lean-tos at the far end of each pair difficult. A plan of the houses, which may date from about the time of their building, shows that each dwelling in the pair had a square front living room with a large hearth on the dividing wall and an oven at the inner corner of the stack, a

[79]*H.M.C. 15th Rep.* Appx. part vi. 85.
[80]H. Walpole, *Aedes Walpolianae*, 1747, p. 70; NRO, DS/489/351 x 3, f.18.
[81]Broome, *Houghton*, p. 24.
[82]Houghton, F/1, 2, 3.
[83]CUL, Cholm. 23/2.

small square back room with no hearth, and a staircase at the outside back corner. The two houses without lean-tos on the left of B.22 are in the original state. In 1985 the houses show a variety of window and door arrangements; most of the lean-tos have been removed, but in two blocks the main hipped roof has been lengthened to cover the lean-to. There is also a variety of attachments and outbuildings at the back of the houses, many of which had been added by the 1880s. Most of the doors have been moved to the gable-ends. The houses are all of brick, whitewashed, with dentellated cornices and blue pantiles; the tiles probably dating from after 1800, since Hill colours the roofs light brown pink.

PLATE IV. B.23. THE KING'S HEAD INN. *Formerly New Inn, now Hall Farm. House 4⅝" long. Viewed from the north.*

The New Inn was built by the west side of Rushmoore Way, a road going in the direction of Harpley Dams in 1720. It was part of the new village building programme, and was completed and glazed in January 1736/7.[84] The Earl of Oxford put up there in 1737.[85] It was a significant building, since, until 1800, the main entrance to the park was opposite, between two small square lodges. The drawing shows an imposing building of five bays, the central bay having a pediment, a segmental window in the second storey, and dentellated quoins. It is a double-pile house, with a full-width lean-to at either end, that at the right-hand end, to judge from its slatted windows, probably being a brewhouse or dairy. Two undated maps of Houghton probably drawn in the 1730s show the lean-tos or wings not extending the full width of the house. They also show the building behind the house as a stubby cruciform shape, very like a barn, and the third range is rectangular with a slightly protruding centre section. These buildings do not appear on the drawing. The upright object on the left of B.23 may be a pump, though no handle is shown. The house remained an inn until after 1832, but between that date and 1845 it became Hall Farm.[86] The house looks much the same in 1985 as it did in 1800.

PLATE V. C.1. THOMAS RODWELL, TENANT. *Now Heath House Farm. Oval 5½" × 3¾". Viewed from the south-east.*

Tall three-storey central range with pantiled shallow-pitched roof. In 1985 the house still has much the same shape, although the long low window and the other ground-floor window have been replaced by a single window, and the middle window upstairs has been blocked. The south wall has been rendered. Small windows have been added to the east end of the main range. The material is brick, dull red and weathered to brown, laid in English bond. There was no house here in 1600, and this house must date from the first half of the 18th century, perhaps as late as the enclosure of 1740.

On Map II the house is the larger of the square buildings in the corner of C.1. The road eastwards had been diverted to the north side of the house before 1824. The large barn at C.26 is still there — a fine flint and brick building, with a steep pantiled roof, large tumbles, and a square honeycomb airhole in the south gable. This must date from the first half of the eighteenth century, and is almost certainly not the building shown in C.1, which has air-slits at three levels and a smallish door at either end of the east front. From the angle of the drawing this building ought to be the more northerly of the two smaller buildings at C.26, part of which may remain in the present farm building opposite the house, which has a wall mainly of flint and brick but containing a few irregular lumps of Whitby stone from Houghton Hall. The wall between the house and the other building in the drawing is of large blocks coloured light brown; the present roadside wall is of brick, which could be of the eighteenth century. Note the exposure of rock in the foreground, a feature which also occurs in a.1 but which is not necessarily an accurate record.

PLATE VI. D.1, 2 & 3. EDMUND HOLLAND, TENANT. *Church Farm and cottages. Oval 5½" × 3¾". Viewed from the north-west. Walls brownish-white.*

D.1. Farmhouse on left. Pantiled roof, dentellated quoins to south-west corner of the house and around the windows. On Map III the house is shown as a simple L-shaped building. On the present building this end is of coursed small fieldstones up to eaves level, with dentellated brick quoins that could date from the later seventeenth century; above that the gable is of random flint and brick, probably a rebuild of the nineteenth century. The village store attached to the north

[84]Ibid. 23/3.
[85]*H.M.C. Portland MSS.*, vi. 66.
[86]Houghton, Maps 25 and 26; Broome, *Houghton*, p. 23.

side of the house has replaced the lean-tos. The south front of the present house is brick, of two builds, the east end probably slightly later than the west. The barn on D.1 has an uncrested thatched roof with heavy stumpy crosses, of brick or stone, at each peak, and dove or owl holes in the gable; the full height double doors are undivided horizontally. This barn had been demolished by 1838. Beyond on D.1 is the pantiled roof of a continuation (the joint is clearly shown on Map III), and a low pantiled building is attached to the nearer end. The present barn is of brick, but the west end is coursed fieldstones with some courses laid sloping, and at the north-west corner fossil tumbles of the early eighteenth century. This must be the gable end of the tiled barn on D.1.

D.2. The longish cross-range at the end of the barns on Map III must be the cottage and single-storey range at the centre of the drawing. The cottage has end stacks, a pantiled roof, and three small dormers with flat roofs; the door, just off centre, is of rail-and-panel construction, and has an arched fanlight divided by two shallow curved bars, giving it a Gothick look.

D.3. Further right, this has a similar door to D.2, and beside it is a Gothick window with simple Y tracery. This cottage also has a pantiled roof, but there are no dormers visible and the attic is lit by a small window in the gable, over the lean-to. The gated track between D.2 and D.3 leads to a small yard at the back of the barns. Not shown on the drawing is another building east of the house, which could be a further barn or a cattleshed.

The map of 1600 shows that the whole area to the south-east of the church was then divided very differently. On or near the site of D.1 was a house, gable-end to the road but not actually on it, with axial stack, central door, and indications of upper-floor windows. Two smaller houses, parallel to the road, and a tiny featureless building stood on or near the sites of D.2 and D.3. None of these buildings is readily identifiable with the buildings of 1800; the outside of D.1 could date, basically, from the seventeenth century, but D.2 and D.3 appear to be cottages of the second half of the 18th century. The tithe map of 1838 shows little alteration from 1800, but D.2 and D.3 have now gone.

Note the odd relationship of man, horse, and tumbril.

PLATE VII. D.25. BARN YARD AND BARN PIECE. *Now Fieldbarn Farm. From stack on left to right end of cottage 8″ long. Viewed from the south-west.*

Cottage: symmetrical double cottage of 1½ storeys, with attic window in right gable. Pantiled roof, with lean-to at either end, the right-hand one having a shed door.

Barn: large pantiled roof, sweeping down over projecting wings (cf. Plates XXXII, XL, LXII and LXVIII). Between the wings are full height double doors, not halved. The wings have shed-type doors. The detached building to the right of the barn has a pantiled roof and a small square window in the gable. At each end of the barn is a long corn or hay stack with wrapover thatch. The wall between the barn and the cottage is brown and of large blocks, but the wall stretching to the left side of the drawing is smooth and probably of brick. The windmill in the background is on Map III at the west end of the small piece of land between D.8 and D.9; it belonged to Mr. Humphrey, miller. In 1600 this whole area was open field, and all the buildings on D.25 are probably a post-1740 development.

PLATE VIII. D.27. BELL'S HOUSE. *House and outbuildings 4½″ long. Viewed from the north-east (road).*

This must be the small L-shaped building, and the outbuilding stands against the road. The larger L-shaped building is not drawn and is probably a barn.

The house has a pantiled roof. The straight joint just left of the door suggests an addition to a house that originally had gable stacks, but it is also possible that the right-hand part has been added to a fragment of an older building. The right side has a string course between ground and first floor, and there is another string course on the gable between the eaves. In the peak of the gable is a round or oval tablet, perhaps recording a date. This part of the house looks *c.*1680-1730. At the gable-end a wide ladder reaches in a curious Hogarthian false perspective to a timber support, presumably as access to a door in the 1½-storey lean-to at the back of the house. The left hand end of the house has a large latin-cross window at mezzanine level, and no obvious use or indeed date for this end can be suggested (for a window in a similar position see Plates LII and LXII). The outbuilding on the right appears quite tall, as the outshut at the near end has two storeys; perhaps it is a brewhouse or bakehouse range. The shed has boarded walls and roof. The wall in the foreground is brown and smooth, suggesting brick. There was a house on the same alignment in 1600, but nothing in D.27 suggests a house of this age. It had probably gone by 1838.

PLATE IX. D.28. BIRD'S COTTAGE. *Cottage $1\frac{1}{8}''$ long. Viewed from the south.*
Tiny cottage; rough thatched roof with shallow cresting and dip and possible barge-boards. If there is an attic room it must be just a sleeping-loft. There is no window visible in the heated end of the house, although there could have been one on the north side. The right end of the building has a pantiled roof. Map III shows two buildings on the site: the house is the larger. The map of 1600 also shows two buildings — tiny cottages with axial stacks and central doors — but the one closest to the site of D.28 is at right angles to the road. Apart from this, D.28 is a typical cottage on maps around 1600. It does not appear on the tithe map of 1838.

PLATE X. D.30. COTTAGE. *Cottage $1''$ long. Viewed from the south (although Map III shows its front immediately against the road).*
As with D.28, the attic must be a sleeping-loft under the pantiled roof. The map of 1600 shows a similar cottage but at right angles to the road. There is a building in this position on the 1838 tithe map but it has now gone.

PLATE XI. E. JOHN DRAGE, TENANT. *House $2\frac{3}{4}''$ long. Viewed from the west (road).*
E is not located on Map III, but the tithe map of 1838 shows that John Drage occupied a cottage, shop, and garden at the squat T-shaped building just to the north of D.1, and the letter E has accordingly been placed there. White's *Directory* of 1836 gives John Drage, grocer and draper; he also had a business at East Rudham.
Pantiled roof, and sign over the door to the right. The shop windows have small panes and heavy glazing bars but no shutters, although the small windows in the domestic part have single shutters. Old Rose Cottage, the flint and brick house now on the site, looks the right shape; there is a blocked door towards the north end and the front has been raised by a few courses of brickwork, but it is not easy to discover Drage's shop in what is there.

PLATE XII. F.1. KING'S HEAD – WILLIAM KNOWLES, TENANT. *Oval $5\frac{1}{2}'' \times 3\frac{1}{2}''$. Viewed from the east (road).*
Pantiled roof with flat-roofed dormers. The large main windows have strong bars and shallow-arched lintels. The sign is on the wall at first-floor level. There is an angled fence or tying-rail of four posts and a cross-piece in front of each window. The lower range has a manger attached to the wall. In the pantiled roof is a slatted dormer with a sloping roof. Map III shows a small wing projecting from the middle of the back side. The six buildings to the left of F.1 on Map III are the house and buildings of O.1. The map of 1600 shows a building of much the same appearance on the site of F.1: dwelling-house/inn on right, but with axial stack; central door between windows; slightly lower range on the left. That map also shows that the gate on the right of F.1 was on a track that went through the fields and eventually joined the Docking Way. The house on F.1, however, appears to be a typical eighteenth-century inn (cf. Plate LXXII). The tithe map of 1838 has the same plan but with the addition of a small building to the left of the stable range. This is probably the flint and brick building standing just south of the present King's Head; the bottom three courses are large limestone ashlars, but the whole thing looks post-1800. The King's Head was totally rebuilt in the later nineteenth century — the date 1860 on the south wing looks right for the whole building.

PLATE XIII. F.8. COTTAGES. *Two cottages, $6\frac{1}{4}''$ from left end of the barn to the right end of the second cottage.*
Cottage and barn on left: pantiled roof, two flat-roofed dormers. A pair of $1\frac{1}{2}$-storey cottages with gable stacks, the right one massive. Perhaps built as a small farmhouse, and the left end converted to a cottage after the enclosure of 1740. The attached barn, not a common feature in surviving houses in the county, has double plank doors, undivided, and a small finial on the left gable. There are two air-slits. Map III shows that the cottage is wider than the barn, probably having a lean-to at the back.
Cottages on the right: $1\frac{1}{2}$ storeys, with two axial stacks and rough thatch; two underthatch dormers. The lean-to on the left is dilapidated, with the rafters showing and evidence of timber-framed construction (cf. Plate LXXVIII). In the drawing the cottage itself has a timber-framed look.
The map of 1600 shows the triangular enclosure, obviously an encroachment on Upgate Green, divided into four narrow strips with hedges; at the east end of each strip stands a cottage, all with axial stacks and fronting the road. The two most northerly are very close, and could be the right-hand building of F.8. The present cottage on the site is brick and must date from

*c.*1840 since it is not on the tithe map of 1838. The left-hand cottage and barn of F.8 has nothing in the drawing to suggest that it is older than the eighteenth century. In 1985 there were two two-storey cottages that could be this building. The more northerly is of flint, with dentellated brick dressings, a blocked door and traces of two blocked upstairs windows, and a flint extension to the south. Some of this must be before 1800. Both gables have been rebuilt in brick in a slightly fancy style that suggests *c.*1840. The more southerly building is a pair of cottages, the northern half of flint and brick chequered, the southern of rough-coursed flint. The two halves would correspond to the cottage and barn, but the 'barn' half has no trace of the large doorway. A possible solution is that the southernmost cottage range is the left-hand building in F.8, with the barn, perhaps in chalk or clay lump in 1800, rebuilt in flint to form the second cottage. This would leave the right-hand building of F.8 to be represented by the older fragments in the more northerly of the two described above, while the brick cottage of *c.*1840 stands on a site not occupied in 1800.

PLATE XIV.   G.1. ROBERT SPARROW, TENANT. *Length from barn to barn 4⅛″. Viewed from the south-west (road).*
    The 1½-storey house has a central stack which is either an agglomeration of different builds or is an attempt to draw a stack of two or three flattened hexagon shafts, typical of the period around 1600 (cf. Plates LIII, LVI, LXIV and LXV). Pantiled roof, with a small cross or finial on the left gable. It is just possible that the line underneath the gable-edge is meant to depict a fossil gable, or perhaps a difference of material, although Hill does not normally go in for this degree of refinement. The far side has a lean-to which on Map IV extends less than half the length of the back wall. The ground-floor window could well be a mullioned window of *c.*1600. Three buildings stood here in 1600, all with gable-ends to the road; that closest to the site of G.1 had a central stack and two storeys of windows in the gable-end. The building on the left in G.1 has a small cross on each gable, and the door, window, and slatted window all high in the walls suggest that it may be a granary or an animal-house with an upper storeroom. The building on the right is lower but also has an upper floor. On Map IV an L-shaped building stands behind the house, but this is not shown on the drawing. The small boarded building in the foreground is probably a kennel. Note the wide, rough verges and the cart-ruts. The fence by the house is wooden paling. The tithe map of 1838 shows only two buildings, joined at the corners to form an L. The site is now empty.

PLATE XV.   H.1. MARTHA BARKER, TENANT. *Now Moor Farm. Oval 5½″ × 3¾″. Viewed from the south-east.*
    Map IV shows that the house has a wing at the back of the left-hand gable-end. The open barn and the hut, possibly a privy, behind the house are not on Map IV, and three buildings on Map IV to the south and south-west of the house are not shown on the drawing, while the pond in the foreground is not on the map.
    This is a long 2½-storey farmhouse with pantiled roof and two gabled dormers. There is an attic window in the right gable. The latin-cross window downstairs has shutters to the larger lights only. The lean-to at the left is perhaps a privy. The present house presents the same facade with some alterations: all windows have been modernised, a door has taken the place of the centre ground-floor window, the left-hand door has been blocked, and the house has been extended to the left for a further two bays. The apparent straight joint in the centre of H.1 now appears as a brick pilaster; the right end of the front has a dentellated cornice, and the brick of this end is slightly more orange than the brick of the left end. A straight joint in the right-hand gable-end shows that the whole facade has been butted on. The roof has been raised by about five feet and now encloses both stacks.
    The stable building on the left in H.1 has a pantiled roof, long slatted windows on two floors, and three undivided doors. It is now a cottage, and is of flint with brick dressings, a fact not apparent in H.1. The map of 1600 has two cottages on this site, but neither resembles nor is in the position of H.1.

PLATE XVI.   H.5. BLACKSMITH'S HOUSE. *Length 3½″. Viewed from the south-west (road).*
    Thatched and pantiled roof, and dormer. The domestic part has a massive axial stack. Next left is one bay with ruinous thatch, a dormer door, and an outhouse-type door on the ground floor. The left end has two small windows in the gable and was probably in domestic use, and attached to it is a thatched open-sided lean-to. A small cottage stood gable-end to the road here in 1600. The smithy is at H.24 and is not drawn. This arrangement was still in force in 1838, when

J. Shilling was the blacksmith and wheelwright. A modern house now stands on the site of the smithy, and the cottage on the site of H.5 bears no obvious resemblance to the drawing.

PLATE XVII. H.9. TOWNHOUSE COTTAGE 2½″ long. *Viewed from the south-east (road).*

Pantiled roof and end stacks, the left one inside a gable with a high parapet. The parapet is either the result of reroofing a thatched roof, or perhaps the gable was part of another house that stood to the left, and the stack was an attached one. A specification for repair of the estate cottages in 1829 gives an estimate for a new roof of pantiles for this cottage, together with repair to the gables, the chimney-shaft, and the floor. It required 500 pantiles and 10 ridgetiles, scarcely enough to reroof the whole house.[87] There is a boarded and thatched lean-to at the right end of H.9. The map of 1600 has a small cottage on this site. There is a building here on the tithe map of 1838, but it may be the present large flint cottage with dentellated cornice and quoins, which cannot be H.9.

PLATE XVIII. H.13. KNACKER'S HOUSE. 3⅞″ *from left end of house to right out outbuilding. Viewed from south-west.*

This 1½-storey cottage has a pantiled roof with bargeboards. The domestic door is probably that on the left, while the right end is presumably the shop, with a sloping boarded hood to the door. The near corner has dentellated quoins, and a dentellated cornice runs the length of the front. The gable-end bulges curiously, and although this must just be clumsy drawing it might also account for the long hood between the gable-end windows, which could be either to throw off water or catch bird-droppings. At the back, and attached according to Map IV, is a building with a stack and thatched roof, part of which is decayed and discloses roof timbers of an odd and not easily credible construction. A small building behind the house is not shown, but may be the flint and brick single-storey cottage there at present. The map of 1600 shows a cottage with axial stack on the site of H.13, which may well incorporate some earlier work. The house at present on the site has a brick facade that looks later than 1800; the gable-end shown is flint and largely rebuilt, but a small patch at the south-west corner could be a remnant of the bulge of H.13.

PLATE XIX. H.14. CARPENTER'S HOUSE. *House and outhouse 3″. Viewed from east (road).*

Gable stacks, the right mostly hidden behind the tree. Thatch with undulating ridge and large dormer with gable and thatched roof. There is a lean-to with a pantiled roof on the front of the house that may be a shed or a privy, and traces of another lean-to on the gable-end. The low building on the right, with pantiled roof, grey boarded walls, and a pair of plank doors, must be the carpenter's shop. There was a house on this site in 1600 with an axial stack and central door. In 1838 John Shilling, wheelwright, was the tenant (see H.5). In 1985 a decayed pair of flint and brick cottages stood on the site, with a fossilized flint gable with brick edge in the south end.

PLATE XX. H.15. SHOEMAKER'S HOUSE. *House and outbuilding 2¾″ long. Viewed from south-east (crossroads).*

The axial stack has an uneven top — a second added shaft, or even, unusually, a pot. Hipped thatched roof, with a small underthatch dormer. The position of the stack, central to the bay on the right-hand side of the doors, is odd — both ground-floor and attic room must have been cramped, unless the flue is cranked. The little window at the left end could light a larder, as the house is surely too small to be a compressed three-cell building. It is not unlike the small and featureless house on the site in 1600, and it could easily be a survivor from the sixteenth century. The low building on the right has a cross on its gable, a small window closed by a pair of shutters, and two small doors. This must be the shoemaker's shop. A house was on the site in 1838, but it could well have been the brick-fronted double cottage that now stands on the site and bears no resemblance to H.15.

PLATE XXI. H.16. COTTAGE. 2⅝″ long. *Viewed from the south-east (crossroads).*

The stacks are outlined in reddish brown. The thatch appears to overhang the edge of the gable, perhaps accounting for the hipped appearance of the left end. The right gable is propped by a horizontal balk and two posts. The bargeboarded dormers are unusually large for this size of cottage. The falling shutter is also unusual, but this is a long window, suggesting either that the house, or the window, was part of a larger house, or that it belongs to an unnamed craftsman such as a tailor. There is a standard small cottage on the map of 1600. The cottage was still there in 1838, but the house at present on the site is a modern flint building.

[87]Houghton, M.7.p.

PLATE XXII. I. GEORGE BATTERBEE, TENANT. *House and ruin $2\frac{1}{2}''$ long. Viewed from the south-west.*

This house stands on the edge of the moor, south-east of a long pit that in the nineteenth century was reported to be very deep in places. The propped gable-end appears to be timber-framed, with wall posts, centre post, and brace; the prop is against the collar of the roof. The left gable is hipped, and the door is opposite the inset stack. This could easily be the remains of the small featureless building on the site in 1600. The ruin could be clay lump or flint, or even brick — the colour is brown — and may have formed part of the house before 1800. There was no house on this site in 1838.

PLATE XXIII. K. THOMAS CAWTHORNE, TENANT. *House $2\frac{1}{4}''$ long.*

The drawing shows this to be gable-end to the road, but Map IV has it parallel to and fronting the road. It must be viewed from the north-west.

Only the middle section is habitable — note the hole in the thatch near the right-hand end, but note also that the only window in the wall is under the hole. The roof on the left has a strong ridgepiece, with paired rafters of uniform scantling and a simple through purlin under the rafters. There was a small cottage on the site in 1600. The house on the tithe map of 1838 might be this one, but the house on the site in 1985 looks mid-nineteenth century. The present long range of workbuildings running at right angles to the road is not on the tithe map.

PLATE XXIV. L. MRS. BLYTHE, TENANT. *House and rear building $2\frac{1}{4}''$ long. Viewed from the south-east (road).*

This house, with its end stacks and symmetrical facade, looks at first glance like a superior cottage of the late eighteenth century. However, the house it represents, standing on the corner opposite the Old Rectory, presents a much more complicated story. At each end is a fossilized gable of flint fieldstones, with dentellated brick quoins, steep-pitched gable with brick edging and small tumbles, and, in the west end, a midway string course of brick — all marks of a house of around 1700. The west end also has two brick jambs of long, low, seventeenth-century window, blocked by an inserted brick stack. Both fossil gables were raised about 15″ in the eighteenth century by the addition of a brick parapet, and on top of that the front, back and gables have been raised another four feet in brick so that the added parapet is also fossilized. The last raising has a simple double cornice and must have been completed by 1800, for there would not have been room for two full storeys, as shown in L, in the house with the flint gable and small brick parapet. Both cornice and brickwork suggest a date very late in the eighteenth century. The tiled small building behind the house must be the small rear building on Map IV, but the gable-end and stack beyond it may belong to the smithy (H.24), which is not otherwise drawn. The map of 1600 has two small cottages here. The lean-to addition at the back of the present house appears on the tithe map of 1838.

PLATE XXV. M. LUCY KITTON, TENANT. *House $2\frac{3}{4}''$ long. Probably viewed from the north (road), but possibly from the south (churchyard).*

The thatch is very rough. The parapet of the gable is corbelled out on both sides. A cottage with an axial stack stood here in 1600, and its fabric could be preserved in M, which has obviously been three cottages; perhaps the two on the right were modernised in the eighteenth century, although the three-light windows could be earlier than 1700. The house was still there in 1838, but some time after was replaced by the present cottage. If Lucy Kitton is the same Lucy Kitten of P.1, Pond Farm in Bircham Tofts, she must have been subletting this dilapidated cottage.

PLATE XXVI. O.1. THOMAS HEBGIN, TENANT. *Now Town Farm. Oval $5\frac{1}{2}'' \times 3\frac{3}{4}''$. Viewed from the south.*

i. *Main farmhouse.* Pantiled roof, with gables corbelled out. The present house is built of dark browny-red brick of eighteenth-century type, laid in English bond and limewashed. It has a central door, one nineteenth-century window on either side of the door, and a heavy plain three-coursed cornice which is not apparent on the drawing, although the corbels appear the same. There are faint but definite traces of the four windows of the upper storey of O.1 which have been replaced by three nine-light sash windows. The small window in the south gable is now blocked. The gable has four small tumbles in each edge. The nineteenth century alterations must have been accompanied by interior rearrangement. The map of 1600 has two fairly large houses on or near the site of O.1, but nothing in the drawing or the present house looks earlier than 1700. Note the good paling fence enclosing the small front garden.

ii. *Barn.* The present barn has a high-pitched fossil gable of carrstone, with a quartered lozenge in brick at its north end; the main material is flint, with dentellated brick quoins of the seventeenth century in the lower part. A change in masonry shows the level of the front before it was raised. On the south gable-end is the date 1842, but this may only apply to the south end of the barn; the 1838 tithe map shows it exactly the same as Map IVa. The lean-to at the right of the barn in O.1 has been rebuilt. The building peeping round the right end of the barn is the nearer L-shaped building on Map IVa, but the building behind it is not on the drawing.

iii. *The cottage next to the farmhouse* on O.1 has no door to the road, suggesting that it may be part of the farmhouse. The building in this position in 1985 is of split rough-coursed flint with brick dressings and a central door. This must be a nineteenth-century rebuild.

iv. *next right on O.1* is a double cottage with a curiously low small square window near the right-hand end. On or near this site in 1985 is a flint cottage with little resemblance to the cottage in the drawing, but it has a blocked window with dentellated brick surrounds in the south gable, and a fossilized gable in flint at the north end. If this is indeed the cottage in O.1, Hill must have squeezed the buildings together to fit into the oval frame, as he did in other drawings. But it is possible that the present cottage is the featureless building on the extreme right of O.1 which on Map IVa is separated from the other buildings. If this is so the cottage with the central stack is now represented by a small single-storey flint building with a central door and two windows.

PLATE XXVII. O.14. UPGATE PIT COTTAGES. *Whole range 3⅜″ long. Viewed from the east (road).*
All are pantiled. The cottage at the left has corbelled gables, and both the taller cottages have attic rooms of very limited space. The left-hand cottage has a sign over the right-hand door. The one-storey building has slatted windows, suggesting use as a dairy or storeroom. The whole range was apparently still there in 1838; in 1985 the left-hand cottage had gone, but the other buildings survive in a very altered state.

PLATE XXVIII. O.23. COTTAGE. *House 2¼″ long. Viewed from the west (road).*
Really a cottage of 1½ storeys, although there is an upper-floor window. Possibly three cottages, although certainly not built as such — it looks like a conversion of an older house. All the windows are latticed, and the larger ground-floor window looks as if it could be of the sixteenth or seventeenth century. The window at the left-hand end is half blocked. The cottage on the site in 1985 is brick, and dates from the late 1840s.

PLATE XXIX. P.1. LUCY KITTEN, TENANT. *Pond Farm. Oval 5½″ × 3¾″. Viewed from the south.*
Pantiled roof and dentellated cornice. Central door, flanked symmetrically by two and three-division latin-cross windows; rail and panel door. In the house of 1985 the windows have been converted to sashes, using the 1800 openings; the dentellated brick surrounds survive. In actuality the windows are not equally or symmetrically spaced. The window to the left of the door is now a late-Victorian bay. Hill has compressed the length of the house in proportion to its total height by about 25%, although he has got the proportions of roof to wall height about right. The internal stacks on the present house are both axial, but the right-hand stack has been rebuilt from the form shown on P.1, which appears to have divided or even lozenge-shaped shafts. In the east gable-end of the present house there is a large, blocked window with dentellated brick quoins, and two similar but smaller blocked windows on the first floor of the same end. The west gable has the same arrangement above a large post-1800 lean-to, but here one of the attic windows has a label. Both gables have square tumbles of brick, a form that seems to have preceded the triangular tumbles of the early eighteenth century, and the dentellated quoins are of brick of a sixteenth or seventeenth-century type. The facing material is rough-coursed, split, grey-white flint, a fact that the drawing does not attempt to convey except perhaps in the colour, which is white streaked with pale brownish-red.

The house as at P.1 is probably seventeenth-century. The roof is steeply pitched, but the gables do not have the parapets of a thatched house, so it is possible that this may be a very early use of pantiles or, of course, plain tiles, which were in use from the Middle Ages. Against this it could be argued that the cornice on P.1 may indicate an eighteenth-century reroofing. The gable-ends and their fenestration suggest a date early in the seventeenth century. The map of

1720[88] shows the house as a simple long narrow rectangle, so the two small back wings on Map V are likely to have been added between 1720 and 1800. The building on the left in P.1 is shown as a long narrow rectangle on the map of 1720; the heart-shaped figure, probably brick in a flint wall, is typical of the period 1630-1700. The building was still there in 1838, but neither the tithe map of that year nor Map V shows the apparent gabled projection. It was replaced by the present L-shaped building in the nineteenth century. The building on the right of P.1 appears in a very much smaller form on the map of 1720; it was still there in 1838, but only a fragment survives. It is difficult to suggest what the obelisk-like shape in front of this building on P.1 is — it seems to be part of the wall beneath it, and may be simply a decoration. The large barn on Map V at the back of the house but not on P.1 is still there. In 1720 it is drawn as a simple rectangle running north-south; if this is accurate, it had acquired additions by 1800. It is of flint, with a square, honeycomb airhole of brick at the south end. There is a fine set of railings set on a dwarf wall in front of the house in P.1. The present wall of brick pillars is late nineteenth century. The drawing puts the pond too close to the railings, since Map V shows that the road, then as now, runs between the pond and the railing.

PLATE XXX. P.14. COTTAGE. *House 2″ long. Viewed from the west (road).*
  A high, hipped, thatched roof. This could be a two-family cottage with a shared stack. A building of similar shape is on the map of 1720, and P.14 looks as if it could have been built well before that date. The cottage on the site is not recognisable as P.14.

PLATE XXXI. P.22. COTTAGES. *Total length of the two buildings 5¼″. Viewed from the north-west (road).*
i. *Long row on the left.* The stacks and the pantiled roof are pink, and the walls are white with pink dressings — one of the clearer indications in the survey of the building materials. The walls are flint, with dentellated brick dressings, and a dentellated cornice is clearly visible. The small window in the right gable indicates an attic room. There is nothing here on the 1720 map, and the whole range appears to be of the second half of the eighteenth century. The double cottage sharing a stack on the left side was probably the first part to be built; a single cottage and stack was added, and the small, apparently stackless, cottage at the right end, with the lean-to, was completed last. The present building has had its walls raised to full two-storey height in brick, and the former gable shows as a fossil.
ii. The second building is not shown as having flint walls, but the present house has some flint-work in this front, together with a raised upper storey in brick and a fossil gable of fieldstones with a blocked window. It seems earlier than (i), but there is nothing on the map of 1720.

PLATE XXXII. Q.1. THOMAS LOWE, TENANT. *Lower Farm. Oval 5⅝″ × 3¾″. Viewed from the south (road).*
  In contrast with P.1 (Plate XXIX), the proportions of the house are exactly right. The present house is faced with fieldstones and split flints, coursed in the upper storey but uncoursed for most of the ground floor. There are dentellated brick quoins, brick dressings to the windows, and a brick string-course of four courses. The brick quoins on the ground floor level are of seventeenth-century type bricks, similar to those in P.1. The fenestration is the same as in 1800 for the first floor, but the window and door arrangement on the ground floor is completely different. The drawing shows a rail-and-panel door opposite an axial stack (now removed), with a secondary door at the right-hand end. This suggests a three-cell plan. Since 1800 the front wall has been raised about two feet, in brick, and now has a dentellated cornice; the west gable is in English bond brick which must also be of the nineteenth century, although it contains a slight scar of the attic window, which must have been carried through the rebuilt gable. On the map of 1720 the house is a long narrow rectangle with a small square wing at the rear of the west end; the right end is attached to a range that runs to the road. Both the drawing and Map VI show a gap at the right-hand end of the house, and the map also shows a considerable wing at the west end. As drawn, the house is typical of the period 1670-1720; the gable has a deep parapet, and the roof is steep, perhaps suggesting thatch as the original covering. The present roof is of blue pantiles.
  The barn on Q.1 is of the double-winged form that appears elsewhere (cf. Plates VII, XL, LXII, LXVIII). The tall double undivided doors are grey, and the walls have a pinkish tinge. The projecting wings have small doors and airslits, suggesting cattlesheds or stables. Map VI

[88]Houghton, Maps 10 and 11.

shows a projection on the east end of the barn that is not on the drawing. A long narrow building is in the position of this barn in 1720. The tithe map of 1838 does not show the projecting wings, although this does not necessarily mean that they had been removed. The barn is no longer there.

The building on the right of Q.1 is of considerable length, and Map VI shows extensions on the back. The stack suggests a brewhouse, bakehouse, or smithy, or indeed lodgings for labourers, as there were few cottages in Bircham Tofts. The building is still there, although it had been shortened at the north end by 1838; it is of flint with brick dressings, and has carrstone in the lower part of the south gable-end. The west side has a plain three-stage cornice.

PLATE XXXIII. Q.14. COTTAGE ADJOINING INFIELD. *House 2¾″ long. Viewed from the north (road).*

Pair of 1½-storey cottages, with thatched roof and gabled dormer. There is an apparent straight joint to the right of the left-hand door; in spite of the appearance of the roof, it seems likely that it marks the end of the earlier cottage on the right, and that the left end is an addition. There was a rectangular house on this site in 1720, although it does not seem quite as long as Q.14. Note the heavy single shutters. The building at present on the site bears little resemblance to Q.14. It has a flint ground floor and a brick upper storey, and could be a rebuild.

PLATE XXXIV. Q.25. COTTAGE IN CHURCH FIELD. *1⅝″ long. Viewed from the north-east (road).*

Double cottage of almost two storeys. The asymmetrical arrangement of doors and windows, together with the unusual size, for this type of cottage, of the main ground-floor window, suggest that it might be the remnant of an older house. The map of 1720 shows a large U-shaped building occupying the site, but this looks like a range of farm buildings.

PLATE XXXV. Q26. COTTAGE IN CHURCH FIELD. *2″ long. Viewed from the north-west (road).*

Cottage of 1½ storeys. The white walls, shaded grey, suggest flint. The big stack on the right must be attached to the far side of the house. The placing of the door is unusual, as is the complete absence of windows on the side facing the road. The barge-board on the right gable suggests that the house was formerly thatched — the outshut has very rough thatch. There was still a house here in 1838.

PLATE XXXVI. Q.34. COTTAGE IN CHURCH FIELD. *1½″ long. Viewed from the north-west (road).*

The light grey colour of the walls suggests flint, but it could equally well be chalk, clay lump, or timber-framing — note the horizontal marks or cracks. The bedchamber is completely in the roof, the visible windows are small, and the whole of the ground floor appears to be one room with a hearth at the west end. The object on the left is a thatched kennel or fowlhouse. If the position of the gate is right the house must have stood gable-end to the road, an alignment confirmed by the tithe map of 1838. However, the map of 1720 shows a small square cottage standing right against the road, but it is difficult to believe that Q.34 was built as a new house after 1720. The cottage on the site in 1985 bears no resemblance to Q.34.

PLATE XXXVII. Q.40. COTTAGE. *House 2½″ long. Viewed from the south-east (road).*

The whitish colour of the front wall suggests flint or chalk. It seems to be a three-cell house, with the centre and right-hand rooms sharing the stack, and the left-hand room unheated. However, the door in the right gable-end suggests either that it was a two-cell house and the right end has been added, or more likely that it is a three-cell house and the end door has been inserted. The stack could be Hill's version of a late-sixteenth century stack with two flattened-hexagon or lozenge shafts (cf. Plates XIV, LIII, LXIV and LXV). The bowed roof with its gable cross looks old, and the shallow parapet gable protecting the edge of the thatch suggests a wall of masonry rather than timber-frame. The horizontal cracks are marked, however, and if they have any significance would suggest timber-framing rather than flint, chalk, or carrstone; it is possible that Hill meant to show barge-boards rather than a parapet gable. The propped left end, with its slatted window, is probably a dairy. There were two buildings on the site in 1720, this house being one of them; the other was larger, and could have been a small barn. The small building at the right front of the house on Map VI can hardly be the boarded kennel of the drawing, and it may be the remnant of the barn of 1720. There is a small building on the site of Q.40 on the 1838 tithe map, but the house on the site in 1985, of re-used brick with some fieldstones in the west gable-end, must be a complete rebuild.

PLATE XXXVIII. R.1. WIDOW BLYTHE, TENANT. *Now The Old House. Oval 5¼″ × 3¾″. Viewed from the east (road).*

The present house is very like R.1, except that the upstairs windows have been raised and renewed. The left side from the central window is flint, split and roughly coursed, and topped with about 2½ feet of dark red brick, which continues through to the north end of the east front. The right end of the front is brick, of a late-eighteenth or early-nineteenth century type. The drawing gives no indication of this change of material, but it could be that the lower part of the north half was refaced after 1800. A small portion of brick window surround appears, fossilised, at the extreme left end of the front; this gives the level of the windows of the drawing, and is compatible with the dentellated brick quoins, which appear to be of the seventeenth century. The present north gable has two small windows, which are not shown on the drawing. The south gable-end of the present house has a bottom half of fieldstones, and an upper half of small coursed carrstone, repaired by brick where the stack has been removed. The small attic window has been renewed. Map VII shows that the back wing of the house is very small. In 1720 the house is shown as a rectangle with a short eastern projection at the north end; this must have stood where the right-hand window is on R.1, and the scar of its removal has been obliterated by the rebuilding of this end in brick. Two small buildings stood to the north of the house in 1720, and four farm buildings to the south. The largest of the latter may be the building on the left of the house in R.1, which has a doveloft in the gable. It had gone by 1838, when the tithe map was made. The building on the right in R.1 is a mixed range of considerable length; the present row of outhouses may be the remains of this building, which does not appear on the map of 1720. Not shown on R.1 is a large winged barn; this is not on the map of 1720, and must have been built in the middle of the eighteenth century when the farms were rearranged. In 1800 the house is approached by a yellow path — sand or gravel — between small lawns.

PLATE XXXIX. R.28. COTTAGE. *Length of house 2¼″. Viewed from the south (churchyard).*

Both stacks are large and rough. The roof is pantiled, and the ridge and gables are emphasised. The partitioned beestand for eight skeps is unusual, but there is another at W.1 (Plate LXIII). The skeps have a large hole near the base, and are probably of straw or basket-work. The map of 1720 shows the house without the projection, but there is a barn and another smaller building to the north, and a small orchard to the east. The house at present on the site has a central stack, probably in the position of the larger stack in R.28; the south front is mainly split grey or white flints, with remains of dentellated surrounds of windows. It was reconstructed in the nineteenth century, probably before 1838, by which time the beestand projection seems to have gone. The west door has been blocked and a new one made, and there is a dentellated cornice. The quoins of the south-west corner are bricks of the seventeenth century, similar to those in R.1. This had undoubtedly been a small farmhouse before 1720.

PLATE XL. R.29. FARM HOUSE. *Length 6¼″ from the left corner of the barn to the right corner of the tall outbuilding. Viewed from the south-east (farm road).*

In 1720 this was the farmhouse of Alice Youngs, one of the larger tenants of that time. The map of 1720 shows the house, with only a single short wing at the back of the west end. Map VII shows two short stepped ranges behind this end. On R.29 the right-hand stack is massive, and the middle stack may belong to a range at the back. The roof is pantiled, and there is a small cross on the right gable. The south front of the present house is largely flint, and a nineteenth century flint and brick wing projects south from the east end. The west front of the present house is also nineteenth-century. As it stands in R.29 the house does not look much older than 1720.

The 1720 map shows a barn in the same position as that of 1800, but without the wings. It is possible that this is, in part at least, the barn of 1800, for although the brick-faced west wall looks late eighteenth century its inside face is flint fieldstones. The short lengths of plain moulded-brick at ground-table level on either side of the west door seem to belong to the brick wall. This great door (not visible on R.29) is blocked, as is the east door shown there between the two wings. The south wing has gone, but its north wall, with two small blocked doors, now forms the south wall of the outshut lean-to, the roof of which also covers the blocked east door. The south wing on R.29 has two small doors high in its wall, a feature that does not occur in the other winged barns in the survey. The building on the right is tall, and has a finial, corbels, and a first-floor door. It could be a granary. There was no building there in 1720. There was a range of buildings on the site in 1838, and some of these still exist in a dilapidated condition. The present high red brick wall between house and yard is the back wall of a post-1838 cartshed. The wall in that position in 1800 could be chalk — one of the existing nineteenth-century farm

148

buildings has a chalk wall. The purpose of the wooden construction on the right of R.29 is not clear.

In 1720 there was another farmhouse with buildings in the occupation of Nicholas Young immediately to the north of this property.

PLATE XLI. R.31. COTTAGE. *House $2\frac{1}{2}''$ long. Viewed from the east.*
This is the larger of the two buildings on Map VII — the smaller must be the lean-to against the wall. The roof is rough thatch, and the gables have deep parapets. All the windows, apart from the lower right-hand one, have been blocked and small openings made in the blocking material in three of them. Two of the upper windows could have been long low windows of Tudor/Stuart type. The single large window has heavy glazing bars, and fills one half of a very large blocked opening. This is obviously a much-altered house in an advanced state of disrepair, and the fact that it has two full storeys suggests that it had once been a house of some importance. On the map of 1720 it is drawn as a rectangular building slightly longer than R.1 (Plate XXXVII). The high yard wall, which is grey, could be chalk or flint, and the lean-to is a shed, fowlhouse, or privy. All buildings had gone from the site by 1838.

The plot between R.1 and R.31 was glebe. The 1720 map has a large E-plan house facing west on the site, with three outbuildings. This was the rectory. None of the buildings had necessarily gone by 1800, for Hill's practice was not to map buildings that were not part of the estate, but the tithe map has only a small building there. The present Rectory House was built later in the nineteenth century, but before 1883.

PLATE XLII. R.32. COTTAGE. *Length of house $2\frac{1}{2}''$. Viewed from the east.*
Double cottage of $1\frac{1}{2}$ storeys. The lean-tos at each end are boarded. Note the double shutter on the small ground-floor window. There was a house here in 1720. The east wall of R.32 can still be seen — chalk, galletted with carrstone, and dressings of seventeenth-century or early-eighteenth-century dark red brick. The building at right angles to the cottage on Map VII is omitted from the drawing, and by 1838 had been replaced by the present brick and flint outbuilding.

PLATE XLIII. R.33. COTTAGE. *House and outbuilding $2\frac{1}{8}''$ long. Viewed from the south-east (road).*
The map of 1720 has a long narrow building on the site that evidently did not belong to Walpole. R.33 is a fragment of a larger cottage or house; the barge-boarded gable suggests that it may be timber-framed, but flint is just as likely. The steep roof is thatched, and the windows are small but indicative of two full storeys. The pantiled building on the right must be a small barn; it does not appear as a separate building in 1720. The cottage was still there in 1838, but the house now on the site is not recognisable as R.33.

PLATE XLIV. R.34. COTTAGE IN BARN CLOSE. *Length $2\frac{1}{4}''$. Viewed from the east (road).*
Double cottage with outshuts, all pantiled except left-hand end. The right gable has a small finial, and in the apex, above a two-light window, is a lozenge which may be either a decoration or a datestone. The cottage on the site in 1985 is very much done up; the bottom two-thirds of the east face are of large blocks of chalk or limestone, and above that is about five feet of miscellaneous brickwork and a dentellated cornice.

PLATE XLV. S.1. THOMAS HERRING, TENANT. *Now Manor Farm. Oval $5\frac{1}{2}'' \times 3\frac{3}{4}''$. Viewed from the south.*
On the map of 1720 this is an L-shaped building, the foot of the L being a short wing projecting south from the west end. Map VIII shows that the west wing projects beyond the line of the back wall of the right-hand range, and there is another projecting wing behind it, to which the centre of the three stacks may belong. This is a large and impressive farmhouse, partly modernised by 1800 — note the two sash-windows by the road. The door at the junction of the gable and the right-hand front is in an odd position, but it may be a drawing fault. The present house has a west end that is flint for the right-hand two-thirds and eighteenth-century brick for the rest. The five windows are in the positions shown on S.1, but there are also remnants of dentellated brick surrounds of long low windows of early-seventeenth-century type on both floors in the flint portion. The south corner of the house has a four-step moulded brick corbel halfway up the wall, supporting a shallow brick projection. There are dentellated brick quoins

to match the fossilized window surrounds. The brick portion of the west end is probably a rebuild of the later eighteenth century, but the north end wall, under the left-hand stack in S.1, is a mixture of brick and flint, and has the course of the flue traced in the wall by horizontal bricks, a feature sometimes seen in Tudor-Stuart farmhouses. The south end-wall of this range has rather fussy Victorian-looking flintwork to about eight feet, and above that, brickwork of perhaps the early eighteenth century, with tumbled gables and a steep-pitched roof. There is no sign of the door on S.1. Perhaps the short wing on the 1720 map stood here to first-floor level. The other wing of the present house faces south-east and is brick; it looks early eighteenth century, with some later alterations. There are fossil lintels of four windows and a door to the right of the centre of the range, but they do not correspond to anything on S.1.

The building on the right of the drawing has a hipped, or possibly a mansard, roof; Map VIII shows shallow wings on the east side. There was a building in this position in 1720. On the left of the drawing is an open timber-framed cart-shed. Neither building is on the tithe map of 1838. On Map VIII a long irregular barn stands east of the house, but this is not shown on the drawing. It was still there in the same form in 1838.

PLATE XLVI. S.26. BASSAM'S PIGHTLE. *House 2″ long. Viewed from the south-east (road).*
Although there is no sign of the road, this must be the south view. A pantiled double cottage with an unusual window arrangement, this looks like a building of the later eighteenth century, although there is a house on the site on the map of 1720. The odd structure at the left end is probably a shed with a bundle of hay on the roof. The house is still there, but has considerable additions of the nineteenth century at the east end.

PLATE XLVII. S.27. PEARSON'S HOUSE. *House and barn 2⅜″ long. Viewed from the north-east.*
A two-bay house with entry in the stack bay. The stack is massive, and the entry must have been cramped. The two large windows and the smaller one upstairs are mullioned and latticed, with diamond panes, suggesting an origin in the sixteenth or seventeenth century. The other window is slatted, and may be the window to the dairy. The emphasised surrounds to all windows suggest that they may be of heavy timber, but the surrounding wall, whitish and streaked brown pink, could be flint or chalk. The house standing here in 1720 was rather longer, having perhaps another cell on the left side of the stack to make it a three-cell house. On Map VIII the barn is shown to be parallel to the house. Its visible wall has five vertical studs; the infill is grey-brown, and could be either sunken daub or boards nailed to the inside of the studs, both of which would be unusual. The house and barn are both thatched, but the lean-to on the barn is tiled, and is post-1720. The yard wall is large, brown, heavy blocks, suggesting stone rather than brick or flint. The cornstack appears to be round, in contrast to the few others in the survey, which are oblong and without the sharp crest. The National School, built in 1845, is on the site of S.27.

PLATE XLVIII. S.47. BLACKSMITH'S HOUSE. *Total length of buildings 2″. Viewed from the north-west (road).*
Pantiles and thatch. The centre house is of typical sixteenth or seventeenth century form, with high-pitched roof and small gabled dormer. The block on the right looks like a late-eighteenth century addition, although a range of similar size is on the map of 1720. The forge on the left has a large door for the entry of horses, a small two-light window, another with slats, and a small window with closed shutter. The right end is brick and is still there. Next left is a cottage with flint walls up to full two-storey height. The forge has been completely rebuilt.

PLATE XLIX. S.50. OVERTON FOX'S HOUSE. *Length 1⅝″. Viewed from west across pit.*
The right end is a two-cell form typical of the Tudor-Stuart period, with massive stack and bargeboarded dormer. The ground-floor window, with its shallow arched lintel, is of the late eighteenth century, and there is a straight joint between it and the left-hand end of the house, which has a shed-type door and could be timber-framed or clay-lump. The thatch is rough, with little evidence of cresting. The fisherman is typically neckless. This cottage had gone by 1838.

PLATE L. S.65. THE ROSE AND CROWN PUBLIC HOUSE: JAMES STAPLETON. *Total length of buildings 3″. Viewed from south-west (road).*
  The public part of the inn is on the right side. Note the two signs, the smaller perhaps with the innkeeper's name. Map VIII shows a small outshut attached to the back of this end. The

lean-to with its low stack could be the brewhouse. The building on the right, if the scale is correct, is probably a pigsty; one door has a square head, the other is rounded. There is a boarded kennel on the left of the drawing.

Apart from a modern porch shielding the door, and windows inserted to the right of the door, the facade is much the same in 1985 as it was in 1800. The north end has brick string courses set closely in a flint wall. The whole building looks eighteenth century, and the map of 1720 shows nothing on the site. The lean-to and the building on the right of S.65 were replaced by the present outbuildings after 1838.

PLATE LI. S.67. THOMAS GENT, TENANT. *House and ruin 3¼" long. Viewed from the north (road).*
The house is the smaller of the two buildings on Map VIII. The thatch is very rough and uncrested, and there is a tiny under-thatch dormer. A massive stack leaves the baffle entry very cramped. The map of 1720 shows this building to be rather longer, and it could be the remains of a three-cell house; from the barge-board and the exposed timbers it could well be timber-framed. The left end has a straight joint and a large vertical crack, possibly by a main post, and this end is unheated. The ruined building also appears on the map of 1720, and its wide door and airslits show that it was a barn. The track on the left leads to Harpley Dam Field. There is an early-nineteenth-century brick cottage on the site.

PLATE LII. T.1. EDMUND WALKER, TENANT. *Lower Farm. Oval 5½" × 3¼". Viewed from the south-west.*
In the drawing the house appears to stand gable-end to the road, but Map IX shows that in fact it ran parallel to it, and the road itself is not, and has never been, curved.

The house has a pantiled roof, using the convention that Hill employs for the tiled roofs of other houses in Harpley. The dentellated cornice would make it eighteenth century, but this might date from a re-roofing. The farmhouse on the map of 1720, then in the occupation of Geoffrey Brown, is drawn as a simple rectangle in the position of T.1. The left end of T.1 has two large twelve-light windows with heavy glazing bars, flanking a tall 24-light window. This is surely a stairlight, unless the whole of the end is an open hall rising through two storeys; but it would also be unusual to have a stair in this position. Map IX shows this end of the house to be quite narrow. In the centre right is a porch, approached from the gate on the left by a path. Map IX suggests that the low building with the gable stack is attached to the right front of the house. Also according to the map, the largest of the outbuildings on T.1 stood well to the right and behind the axis of the house, and a barn and two other outbuildings behind the house have been omitted, unless the large building on T.1 is meant to be the barn. The small building on the extreme right appears to be a coach-house or cart-house, although there seems to be little room to manoeuvre a vehicle. Most of the outbuildings were added after 1720, presumably with the consolidation of several small farms. The covered wagon on the road is probably a carrier's wagon, with two small wheels in front of the two large ones shown.

The house of 1800 remains as part of the present house; the dentellated cornice is still there, but the fenestration has been completely altered, and the range now has no stacks. A solid Georgian-style wing stands across the north end — as this is not shown on the tithe map of 1838 it presumably dates from the middle of the nineteenth century. The two small buildings on either side of the entrance are still there, though altered. There is a long barn behind the house.

The 1720 map shows a group of buildings on the other side of the road opposite T.1, and further south on that same side is a curious H-shaped building with a small orchard behind it. On the same side of the road as T.1 the map of 1720 shows four small buildings standing by the road at the ends of strips in the position of T.4, 5 & 6.

PLATE LIII. T.20. COTTAGE. *House 1¾" long. Viewed from the north-east.*
The stack has two lozenge or flattened hexagon shafts on a square plinth, and must date from the sixteenth or early seventeenth century. The gables have round-topped parapets, and the left-hand gable has a corbel with a short finial. The left-hand window has three lights and a sixteenth century type label or dripstone. The part of the house to the right of the door could have been rebuilt. On the 1720 map the building on the site of T.1 looks longer than the house in the drawing. The house had gone by 1838.

PLATE LIV. T.21. PELL'S COTTAGE. *House and ruin 3¼" long. Viewed from the south (road).*
1½-storey cottage with heavy rafters showing through the holes in the rough thatch. There is an L-shaped building on the site on the 1720 map, with the foot of the L going back from the

right-hand end as seen on T.21 — the gable here may have been rebuilt when the wing was demolished. An estimate was made for repairing the roof of this cottage in 1829,[89] and a small house, probably this one, is shown on the tithe map of 1838. There is no house here in 1985, but the fossilised remains survive in the brick wall of the orchard. The ruin in T.21 is the remnant of a larger house of at least six bays, with a massive tapered stack opposite the door; it must have been a three-cell house, with the left end unheated. As no traces of a timber frame remain it could be of chalk or flint; the slight fossils of a brick building appear in the high north wall of the orchard of Lower Farm, but these could be from a nineteenth-century garden building. There is no building on the 1720 map in the position of the ruin, so it could have been uninhabitable even then, when the main house was in the occupation of John Lewis. The 1720 map has a small farmstead by the road in T.16, two small buildings to the north of that, and two more small cottages at the road-ends of enclosed strips in T.17.

PLATE LV. T.39. HOUSE, BARN. *Total length of barn and house 5⅝″. Viewed from the north (road).*
In 1720 two buildings stood exactly on these sites. There was an orchard behind, and the occupier was Edward Springal. The three-cell house of T.39 is obviously a farmhouse that has suffered the common fate of conversion to cottages. The smaller cottage, on the right, probably has one room up and one down and shares the stack with the larger cottage. This has the original doorway opposite the stack; the large room in the centre of the range, the former 'hall', now has two windows and, of course, the hearth, while the room on the left is unheated. There is almost a full storey upstairs, and the thatch has cresting. The right-hand gable has a parapet, but there may be a barge-board on the left-hand gable. The house could be at least part timber-framed. The barn has deep parapetted gables, and there is a small finial on the left. There is a lean-to behind the thatched part. The exposed roof has a heavy ridge-piece and coupled rafters of uniform scantling, with a simple through-purlin under the rafters (cf. K Plate XXIII). There are tall, paired doors, divided horizontally. Both house and barn could date from at least the seventeenth century. The tithe map of 1838 shows a house on this site, but the barn is not there. A small brick house with dentellated cornice now stands by the roadside on or near the site of the barn.

PLATE LVI. U.1. JOHN YOUNG, TENANT. *Hall Farm. Oval 5½″ × 3¾″. Viewed from the west.*
This is perhaps the most interesting and complicated house in the survey. In the drawing, both gables have coping, corbels and small finials. The slope of the roof is quite sharp, but the roofing material is certainly not thatch. Hill uses this convention on six other houses, with variations. U.1, W.26 (Plate LXVII) and X.1 (Plate LXVIII) have strong horizontal lines but no vertical lines; U.22 (Plate LIX), W.23 (Plate LXIV) and X.53 (Plate LXXII) have horizontal lines with short vertical dashes in an alternating pattern; and V.1 (Plate LXII) is similar to the latter, but the vertical lines are more irregular. In none of them can the convention represent pantiles, and indeed in Plates LIX, LXIV, LXVII, LXXII and LXII Hill shows pantiles in his usual convention and normal, reddish, colouring. The colour of all these roofs is light grey, and the convention looks most like slate. Although there were plenty of stone slates, tiles, and slabs available in eighteenth-century England there is little evidence for their use in Norfolk, and the same can be said for true slate from the west country, the north-west, and Wales. However, Welsh-type slate became popular in the nineteenth century, and it may be significant that Hill shows Dersingham church, in Plate LXIII, roofed in the same convention as the houses listed above: the present roof of the church is grey slate. Neither plain tile, because of the colour, nor lead, because of the cost, are likely alternatives for the roofs of these houses. Welsh slate for the roof of an important farmhouse like U.1 is understandable, but it is not easy to account for its use on the other buildings. The slate roof of the present Hall Farm was put on about eighty years ago, but in any case, as we shall see, it is not the same roof as Hill drew.
Whatever the roofing material, the rest of U.1 is also interesting. In the centre of the roofline an axial stack, removed in recent years, carries three lozenge or flattened hexagon shafts. The stacks on the west side each carry two similar shafts, and at the peak of the south gable is a single shaft of the same form. The flattened hexagon is quite common in the county and usually dates from the later sixteenth century. Other examples are at G.1, T.20, W.23 and W.24 (Plates XIV, LIII, LXIV and LXV).
The north end of the present house is flint and brick. Both corners and much of the lower part of the wall is brick of a medieval type, hard and pink, and the north-east corner is corbelled out

[89]Houghton, M.7.p.

flush with the gable-end at a height of about eight feet. The whole bottom half of the north gable-end looks a genuine late-medieval wall. It contains the fossilised brick surrounds of the two first-floor windows of U.1 as well as the fossil gable-edge, with a single two-brick tumble, and traces, perhaps, of earlier windows. The window openings are blocked with the same medieval-type bricks; spoils, perhaps, of the nineteenth-century rebuilding. A ground-floor window opening, not visible on the drawing, is blocked with large coping-bricks. There is a modern inserted stack. The attached stack at the left end of U.1 has gone, and the absence of a scar suggests that it may have been butted on to an existing wall. There is no evidence of the slight inset visible at the left-hand corner of U.1, and it may be that the wall had been slightly widened before 1800 and then taken back to the original line when the stack was removed, accounting, of course, for the absence of a scar. The narrow lean-to next to the attached stack is still there, and is of sixteenth or seventeenth-century brick, although the upper part was rebuilt with a pitched roof in the early nineteenth century. U.1 shows a door immediately to the right of this feature. The stack further right in this wall has gone, but scars indicate its position and that of the two-storey lean-to against it, which later in the nineteenth century was given a pitched roof and extended westward. It is said to have been used as a schoolroom. The south wall of the present building that stands on the site of this projection incorporates a few limestone shafts and mouldings, either from the church or from Coxford Priory, just over two miles away. In the drawing a porched entrance with lean-to roof stands in the shadow to the right of this building. The whole of the west front of the house was raised several feet after 1800 and partly clad with brick; it is now full of sash windows, but there are fossilised fragments of the windows of U.1 and of others of the long low type of the sixteenth or seventeenth century. The south gable-end now has a wide, tapering half-inclosed stack of two flues. Recent alterations inside uncovered an enormous nineteenth-century cooking-range. The lean-to building shown against this end was a dairy, and was pulled down in the 1980s.

The east front of the present house is of flint and brick. Parts of a plinth of chamfered tudor brick remain. There are several blocked windows, some with dentellated quoins and chamfered sills and lintels. In the centre of the east front is a stubby attachment, the southern half being a small outhouse of nineteenth-century brick and the northern half a porch entrance, with a heavy flattish Tudor arch and a triangular pediment flanked by smooth pine-cone reliefs. The features are set under a wall of medieval-type bricks in a herringbone pattern, and the north wall of the porch is similarly constructed. In the main wall south of this feature is a blocked early-eighteenth-century doorway, and there is another almost at the south-east corner. Both southern corners of the house are built of the hard pinkish medieval bricks that occur at the north end of the house. While it is possible that these may have been cannibalised from another building, (e.g. Coxford Priory, where bricks of the same general type are to be found), their use as quoins appears perfectly genuine. This could mean that the body of the house dates from the late Middle Ages, with the stacks and gables of U.1 and the fossilised 'Tudor' window surrounds marking a modernisation programme of the sixteenth century. The porch certainly looks late-Elizabethan in its features. It is probably the northern of the two small projections on Map X, but the map shows the whole of the east front to be irregular and it is difficult to relate it to what is there today. Another difficulty is that the tithe map of 1842, while showing the west front as on Map X, has the east front completely straight. If this is accurate it can only mean that between 1800 and 1842 the east front was partly rebuilt, perhaps at the same time as the roof was raised and the west front modernised. The porch would then become an antiquarian reconstruction subsequent to 1842.

If the perspective is correct, the building in the background of U.1 is the squat T-shape, the larger and more irregular barn being hidden by the house. By 1842, additions to the T-shaped building joined it to the building east of the entrance gate, which in part seems to date from before 1700. The tithe map also shows more farm buildings to the south of the house. Few of the farm buildings survive.

PLATE LVII. U.14. DYE'S COTTAGE. *House $1\frac{3}{4}''$ long. Viewed from the south (road).*
Like all the Rudham houses in the survey, this has grey walls. Map X shows an outshut at the back. It is probably a double cottage, but it may be that the width of the hearth necessitated a second door. The windows are rough, and there is a boarded kennel. The house on this site was recently demolished.

PLATE LVIII. U.21. COTTAGE. *House $1\frac{5}{8}''$ long. Viewed from the north-east.*
A small three-cell house, with a tiny window in the unheated room at the left end. The other windows are also small. Attic bedrooms, with no visible windows. A house, including some reused limestone ashlars, stands on the site, but it is probably a post-1842 rebuild.

PLATE LIX. U.22. MAY'S COTTAGE. *House 3¾" long. Viewed from the east.*
The 'slate' roof contrasts in form and colour with the pantiled roof of the lean-to. There is a cross on the right gable. This could be a three-bay cottage, with two bays added at the right end. The house is still there, but an axial stack has been added to the right half and both stacks have tall octagonal shafts after the nineteenth-century 'Elizabethan' fashion. Slight alterations have been made to the doors and windows, and the window over the left door is blocked. The house is of brick, in English bond, with a dentellated cornice, and the whole thing looks of the late-eighteenth century.

PLATE LX. U.28. COTTAGES IN GOOD ALE. *Total length of buildings 5¾". Viewed from the north-east (road).*
i. *Building on left.* The wing at right angles is dilapidated with a dip in the thatch and a large crack in the wall; it has a wide bargeboard and weather-boards in the gable, with a small door giving access to the attic — evidently a cottage converted to non-domestic use. The building was still there in 1842 in the same form. The house there in 1985 has been much renovated, but the south gable-end has an overall diaper pattern of brick in flint of the seventeenth century, and the stacks (an axial one has been added) have tall lozenge shafts of the middle of the nineteenth century.
ii. *Short three-cell thatched house* with one upper-floor window and a flat-roofed dormer. It was still there in 1842 but has now gone.
iii. *Building on right.* The exposed gable shows heavy timber-framing. The centre section of the range is in ruins, and the near end has a hipped thatched roof and is being used as an outbuilding. The tithe map shows a domestic building on the site of this range in 1842, but the building there now, though incorporating some flint and brick remnants, is not readily identifiable with U.28. The tithe map also shows another occupied house between i and ii. The fragment in the foreground of U.28 consists of large blocks which could be chalk or clay lump. The whole group may have been the dwellings of smallholders or manorial tenants of the pre-enclosure period on the site of an early-medieval settlement.

PLATE LXI. U.29. COTTAGE. *House 2¼" long. Viewed from the south-east.*
The lurching, thatched roof is hipped at both ends, and has a flat-roofed dormer with a closed shutter. The left end is very dilapidated, with wide crack, window missing and the wall underneath collapsed. Nevertheless, the left end seems to be inhabited. There is a straight joint between the central window and the right-hand door. The right end is probably one ground floor room and an attic, and the wall here, too, is heavily cracked. The material is probably flint (or possibly clay lump or chalk); it is not likely to have been timber-framing. Map X shows two buildings, both gable-end to the road, although the survey refers only to one. The tithe map of 1842 shows these two with a small building between their east ends, and another stubby L-shaped cottage at the north end of the plot. None of the buildings on the site looks like U.29.

PLATE LXII. V.1. RICHARD STANTON, TENANT. *Ling House Farm. Oval 5½" × 3¾". Viewed from the west.*
The roof is blue-grey, and is drawn in a way not unlike U.1 (see notes on U.1 for detailed comments). It certainly contrasts with the pink pantiles of the farm buildings. The dentellated quoins, the latin-cross windows, central door and end stacks suggest a date between 1680 and 1730, but the break in the line of the eaves and the odd window arrangement at the left end may show that this front is a rebuilding, or cosmetic treatment, of an earlier house. The map of 1693[91] shows the rear or east elevation of the house; it has a gable stack at the north end, another stack in the roofline almost at the south gable, two full storeys divided by a horizontal line, attic with dormers, and two bays on either side of the central door. In the work of some cartographers of the sixteenth and seventeenth centuries the dividing line between floors indicated a jettied house. In 1985 the house on the site has a brick west front, with one wide bay on either side of a central door; a straight joint runs the full height to the left of the door and two of the upper windows show signs of infilling around them, but there is little real resemblance to V.1. Map XI shows a projection on the east side of the house, but comparison with the tithe map of 1839 suggests that the main block of the house may be L-shaped and that the single-storey building on the right in V.1 may be the apparent south wing on Map XI. If this is so, the low building had gone by 1839.
Map XI shows that, in the drawing, Hill has emphasised the size of the house at the expense

[91]Houghton, Map 13.

of the farm buildings. At the left of V.1 is a cottage, forge, brewhouse, or bakehouse with a stack, shown exactly as it appears on the map of 1693. Next is a lower range, and then a barn with a central projecting bay or a shallow porch — the central projection of Map XI. This also is very much as it appears on the 1693 map, which likewise does not make clear the nature of the projection. In 1693 the whole range was some 165 feet long, the length of the range on Map XI less the eastern end. In 1693 another barn range 150 feet long ran northward from the east end of the first barn and had a gabled projection in the centre of its east side. The winged barn of Map XI stands on the site of part of that range, and is not shown on V.1; neither is the stubby L-shaped building. Parts of the farm buildings of 1800 are incorporated in the extensive ranges to the north of the present house.

PLATE LXIII.   W.1. WILLIAM STANTON, TENANT. *Manor Farm. Oval $5\frac{1}{2}''$ × $3\frac{1}{4}''$. Viewed from the north-east.*

Map XII shows the house in the form of a stubby cross, and accordingly the projecting wing on W.1 should be in the middle of the range, with an answering wing on the other side. However, it makes more sense with the wing in the position shown in the drawing. The barn range is obviously compressed, and the church tower is misdrawn so that it appears to stand north of the west end of the nave. The church roof is now slate, and it is interesting to compare Hill's treatment of the roof in 1800 with the way he depicts other roofs in Dersingham and in West Rudham (see notes on U.1). The house has some interesting features: a large two-light window immediately under the stack in the right-hand gable; a bow window at the same end of the house; a nine-light window in the upper floor of the projecting wing; and a three-tier bee-stand in a lean-to at the end wall of that wing (cf. R.28 Plate XXXIX). The roofs are pantiled, but the colour of the walls gives no clue to the material — if they are carrstone Hill would surely have given them a browner hue than the faint brown pink he uses. The tithe map of 1839 shows the house as a strange building: a long south-facing range is joined to a parallel but shorter north range by what appears to be a narrow passage. It is not easy to see how the building of 1800 could become this shape without being entirely rebuilt. The present house is a large double-pile building of carrstone, with red brick dressings, of a similar style to The Feathers (see Plate LXV) and probably dating from the late nineteenth century.

The barn of W.1 has a pantiled roof and a projecting central bay between tall undivided doors. A valuation of 1804[92] says that there were 'two barns, at Home, with two threshing Floors each, and one Barn detached — a large range of Stabling — Another range of Swine Sties and Calf Pens; Two Cart Houses'. The barn here must be one of those with two threshing floors (behind the large doorways) and the other must either have continued on from it in the long shape of Map XII or, less likely, have been the other rectangular building. Neither would leave much room for the rest of the farm buildings mentioned in 1804. The tithe map of 1839 shows a range of buildings about the same length as on Map XII (about 265 feet), but with a single shallow projection in the middle of the east side. This suggests that Hill has drastically simplified and compressed the barn range. The present barn, which must be basically that of 1800, is carrstone with dark red brick dressings, a plain three-stage cornice, and diamond-shaped airholes; the south gable-end is brick with tumbles, and the whole thing looks eighteenth century. Perhaps it was refurbished then, for this is an old-inhabited site, and at the north end of the barn a small attached building has some medieval-type bricks mingled with the carrstone, and there are the vestigial remains of the jamb of a door or a window. Perhaps this is the sole visible remnant of the house in W.1. At the south-east corner of W.22 is a small square building, perhaps incorporated in the present ranges of stables, and at the south-west corner is the tithe barn, a superb small barn of carrstone and brick bearing the date 1671.

W.2 is a walled garden. A high red brick wall forms the east and north sides, and at the north-west corner is a brick gateway of a late seventeenth century type. A similar gateway is in the west wall, in a brick section of what is otherwise a wall of carrstone with bonding pillars of late eighteenth or early nineteenth-century brick. The south wall is a mixture of carrstone, chalk, and brick.

PLATE LXIV.   W.23. HOUSE. *House $3\frac{1}{4}''$ long. Viewed from the west.*

It is not easy to determine the viewpoint. The absence of shadow on the left-hand wall of the tallest range suggests a space between it and the centre building, but comparison with the tithe map proves that it is, in fact, all one. The tithe map shows the dwelling-house to be the building with the projecting wing on Map XII, and its shape fits W.23 much better than that on the map of 1800. We are looking at the west side of the house from the road; the right-hand end faces

[92]Houghton, M.7.n.

south, and its east gable-end, with the stack, is flush with the rear wall of the middle range, while the lowest part is a narrower building, as the position of its roof in the gable of the centre section shows. Hill's drawing is, in this case, more accurate than his plan. The drawing does not include the two other buildings of Map XII, which were probably small farm buildings. The roofs of the larger ranges are grey, in a version of the convention Hill uses at U.1 (Plate LVI), and contrast with the pantiled roof of the left-hand range. Both stacks appear to have flattened hexagon shafts, lozenge shafts being possible but less likely. The stacks, the long low windows, and the heavy dentellated quoins suggest that all three parts date from the sixteenth century. The right-hand range is perhaps the latest; its floor level has to conform with that of the centre section, and as the land slopes away the door has to be approached by three steps. The big latin-cross windows are an updating of the eighteenth century. The building has something of the look of an inn, but it may simply have been the house of a well-to-do yeoman farmer. The valuation of 1804[93] describes this as a 'Dwelling House, let in three tenements'. The early-Victorian school, now the Youth and Community Centre, occupies the site.

PLATE LXV. W.24. COCK PUBLIC HOUSE. JAMES YATES, TENANT. *Length from left fence to right of outbuilding 5". Viewed from the south-east.*
    The roof is pantiled, with a prominent ridge and a cross on the right-hand gable. The stack has two hexagonal or lozenge shafts, as in W.23 (Plate LXIV). These, and the three long low windows, suggest a sixteenth or seventeenth-century origin for the house. All the windows in W.24 have emphasised surrounds, and are latticed with diamond panes. The door on the right of the main building probably led to the cellar or storeroom, and the domestic quarters were probably in the wing at the rear which is not shown on the drawing. The attached outshut has a latticed window, with shutters. The detached outbuilding has a stack and may have been the brewhouse; its wall, of large white blocks streaked with brown, could be meant for carrstone, which is common in Dersingham, but none of Hill's buildings is unmistakably built of this local sandstone. A small, square building in the corner of the pightle is not shown on the drawing. Note the heavy post and rail fence. The house was still there in much the same form in 1839, but the site is now occupied by the Feathers Hotel, a pretentious sub-Sandringham building of dark carrstone and red brick, built sometime between 1861 and 1883.

PLATE LXVI. W.25. GAY'S COTTAGE. *Length of house including lean-tos 4". Viewed from the south-west (road).*
    There is a heavy ridge to the roof, which is reddish in colour and marked in a slightly different fashion from the normal pantiled roof. The small dormers have sloping, tiled roofs. The window towards the right end appears to be blocked rather than shuttered, and next to it is a solid outhouse door with ring handle. Both lean-tos are open and very roughly thatched, and there is a light two-wheeled cart or tumbril at the right-hand end. A tiny mushroom-shaped haystack, presumably part of the product of the pightle, stands in the green foreyard. In 1804 the cottage and pightle were let at £12 a year, the same rent as the Cock and its pightle. The site is occupied by later buildings.

PLATE LXVII. W.26. COTTAGE. *House and lean-tos 2½" long. Viewed from the south-west (road).*
    This has a grey-green roof, with horizontal lines exactly like U.1 (see U.1. for speculation on the material). The left gable has a small knob, hardly a finial. There are two ground-floor rooms, one of them heated, and attic bedchambers. The house may have been replaced by 1839, for the building on the tithe map is much longer than that on Map XII. The site is now occupied by nineteenth-century carrstone and brick cottages.

PLATE LXVIII. X.1. ANTHONY BECK, TENANT. *Abbey Farm. Oval 5½" × 4". Viewed from the north-east.*
    The roof is a version of the convention Hill uses on U.1 (Plate LVI), but here the colour is light grey with a faint brown tinge. The fenestration is odd, and the main door on the right has a low three-light window over the lintel. The small lean-to in the angle could be a shed or a privy. The map of 1730 calls the farmhouse Massingham Abbey and has the house in much the same form as Map XIII, but both wings are slimmer and there is no central projection to the main range. There is little about X.1 to help in dating, and the present house is not very informative. It has a nineteenth-century Georgian three-storey east front of five bays, with a giant pilaster at

93Ibid.

156

either end and cement rendering over the whole; the top storey is brick, and can be seen in the south gable-end sitting on a flint wall, presumably the east front of X.1. This gable contains a medieval doorway and lancet window, either part of, or removed from, the priory. The south wing of X.1 was demolished before 1838 and replaced by the present stable range of flint, brick and reused freestone. The curious building on the left of X.1, with six slatted windows, tiny gabled dormer, and hipped roof in the same convention as the main house, where, however, the dormers are flat-roofed, appears in the same shape on the map of 1730. The building on the site in 1985 is basically of flint with brick dressings, with a brick facade facing towards the green that must be a refacing after 1800. There is a set of doveholes at the west end, and the roof is of pantiles. The original use could have been as a granary. The building on the right of X.1 has a ched roof and an apparently apsidal extension at the east end. It would be fanciful to see this as a remnant of the priory, but a building of similar plan was there in 1730, and it is not easy to explain the rounded end. It had gone by 1838. Behind the house on Map XIII is a large barn, not shown on the drawing, which the map of 1730 shows in a more elongated form. The tithe map of 1838 has three shallow projections to the east.

PLATE LXIX. X.52. COTTAGE. DR. REYNOLDS, TENANT. *House and ruin 1⅝" long. Viewed from the south (road).*
The survey does not make it absolutely clear whether this drawing represents X.52 or X.66, but the former is more likely. If so, X.66 is not drawn. The ruined end shows this to be a timber-framed cottage, originally of two-cell plan and 1½ storeys; main post, bressumer, wall plate, and studs remain, giving the impression of a square box-frame rather than close-studded construction. The three studs at the right end break into this pattern, but they may be insertions. The left end is a flint stack-bay added to the timber-framed cottage; it is coloured grey with dark grey dappling, and the grey quoins might well be freestone robbed from the priory. A simple rectangular building appears on the map of 1730. The site of X.52 is now occupied by an attractive cottage of chequered flint and red brick.

PLATE LXX. X.65. THOMAS MUIR A COTTAGE. *House 1¾" long. Viewed from the east (road).*
A two-bay cottage of 1½ storeys. Both the 1730 map and the tithe map show another cottage butting on to the right end of X.65, but this was presumably not drawn or mapped by Hill because it was not Cholmondeley property. There is at present a cottage on or near the site, but it is not identifiable with X.65.

PLATE LXXI. X.61 and X.64. THOMAS MASON AND JOHN JACKS. THE FOX PUBLIC HOUSE AND SMITH'S SHOP. *Total length of range 4⅝". Viewed from the south-west (road).*
i. *The Fox.* Thomas Mason's inn is on the left, and at the extreme right end of the range is Jacks' smith's shop. On Map XIII the range is undivided, but the garden division between X.61 and X.64 is approximately at the right side of the large stack in the centre of the thatched roof. If this is accurate it would mean that only the right-hand door and window of the thatched house are in the occupation of Jacks, and the rest is part of the Fox property. However, as the written survey makes the Fox property slightly smaller than Jacks', this seems unlikely. Perhaps the tiled range with the bow front belongs to the Fox, while Jacks sublet the left-hand part of the thatched house, which would account for the extra doors. It is also possible that the centre part of the range are not part of the Cholmondeley estate, but in that case one would expect them to be uncoloured on Map XIII, like the attachment at the north end of the Fox. The map of 1730 has a rectangular building on the site of the Fox in the tenancy of William Collings, but there is no indication that it is an inn at that date. The present building, now de-licensed, has a west front of rough-coursed fieldstones, with central door and large shallow-arched windows on the ground floor. The dentellated jambs of the large window on the left of the door in X.61 and of the window above it can be seen as fossils. It is interesting that Hill gives no indication, as he does in Plates LXIX, LXXII and LXXIV, that the main walling material is flint, and it is possible that in 1800 the wall was limewashed. The roof of the present building has been raised after 1800 by about 2½ feet of brickwork, and perhaps at the same time the windows were modernised. What is visible suggests that the building may date from before 1730. The inn sign in X.61 is on a projecting arm above the door. A pheasant was added to the fox in the nineteenth century, and the Mason family continued as licensees until the middle of this century.
The building next to the Fox on X.61 has a separate pantiled roof but no visible stack; perhaps it shared the end stack of the Fox. The whole of the front appears bowed in three planes. The door stands at one of the angles, and the long windows also go round the angles.

The three square lights of the upstairs window are latticed, and there is the suggestion of a blocked fourth light to the left. The facade hides the eaves. The range could be a shop, with a workroom of, for example, a tailor upstairs to account for the large upper window. The brick building now on the site bears no resemblance to that in X.61.

ii. *John Jacks' house and smithy.* There was a building on the site in 1730; it was detached from the Fox building, and perhaps the bow-fronted house is a post-1730 infill. The house on X.64, with its massive central stack and deep thatched roof, looks pre-1700. In 1985 the house on the site has a bland modernised front; there is the scar of a blocked doorway roughly in the position of the left-hand doorway of X.64, but the brick facade is almost certainly post-1800. The smith's shop has a smallish door (cf. Plate XLVIII). Perhaps the open shed with a pantiled roof supported by braced posts was used for the shoeing. The smith in 1838 was Jonathon Jex. The modern building on the site fails dismally to blend in with its surroundings.

PLATE LXXII. X.53. JOHN GAGE, TENANT. THE SWAN INN. *House $3\frac{1}{2}''$ long. Viewed from the south-west (road).*

The map of 1730 has an L-shaped range facing west and south, a long stable range running north-south, and two small buildings at the north side of the yard. The timber-framed right end of X.53 must be part of the building there in 1730. It has a deep jetty supported on seven substantial joists, the walls are heavily cracked, and the two windows on the ground floor have been blocked and single panes inserted in the blocking. The upstairs windows are obviously replacements, perhaps when the main part of the inn was built. The timber-framed end has a roof in the 'slate' convention, coloured grey (see U.1 Plate LVI), and the door is diminutive. Comparison with the map of 1730 suggests that the timber-framed building could be the north end of the old inn, and that the south end, together with the rear wing, was demolished between 1730 and 1800. There is a small featureless attic window in the south gable of X.53. The main house on the drawing looks typical of the second half of the eighteenth century. The right-hand stack has an internal addition, perhaps for a bedroom fireplace. In 1985 the Swan, delicensed, had a rendered front, but otherwise was superficially much the same as in 1800. The timber-framed wing had gone by 1838, but its scar is outlined by plaster on the south gable end of the present building, and on its site stands a nineteenth-century flint and brick building, with a further extension of brick to the south. The exposed gables on the main house are of eighteenth century brick, with small tumbles. The small low structure on the extreme right of X.53 is the projecting wing of the building at the back of the inn. The long building to the south on Map XIII is not shown on the drawing; a building of similar shape appears on both the 1730 map and the the tithe map of 1838. An inventory of goods seized for arrears of rent in October 1742 may apply to the Swan in the timber-framed form before the main house of X.53 was built. The innholder was Thomas Groom, and the rooms listed are kitchen, backhouse, great parlour, long parlour, little boarded parlour, barr parlour, blew room, redd room, green room, nursery, chamber adjoining nursery, and garretts, the last six named rooms all containing beds. Outside were stables and a barn.[94]

The freestanding sign in X.53 is on a brick plinth and has a small 'bush' on its left-hand end.

PLATE LXXIII. X.55. LATE BAXTER'S HOUSE. *The two houses $4''$ long. Viewed from the east (road).*

On the left is a fragment of a two-storey house, with a deep parapet to the left-hand gable and a $1\frac{1}{2}$-storey lean-to at the back. The right half of the house shows irregular timber-framing, probably a box frame with a brace; the inserted door breaks into the pattern. The left half is flint, with uneven quoins ot brick or stone and a massive stepped stack. This looks sixteenth-century, so the timber-framed part could be late-medieval. There is a building of similar plan here on the map of 1730 and on the tithe map of 1838, but the site is now occupied by a house of the late nineteenth century.

The house on the right, separated from the former by a narrow track that leads to the pightle at the rear, is not mentioned separately in the survey. It is a $1\frac{1}{2}$-storey double cottage. A building of the same proportions is on the 1730 map, but if it is the same building it must have been quite new then. The tithe map has a much smaller, square building. The house on the site in 1985 is not recognisably the same building as in the drawing.

[94]Houghton, Red. Box 4.

PLATE LXXIV. X.56. BLACKSMITH'S HOUSE. *House and outbuilding 2½″ long. Viewed from the east (road).*

Map XIII puts the outbuilding behind the left end of the house, but the map of 1730 has it in the position shown in the drawing. This is presumably the smith's shop. The door is not very large, (cf. X.64 Plate LXXI). The stack is in a strange position in the corner of the house, and the placing of the two small gabled dormers is also peculiar. The left end of the front is flint, with large alternating quoins of stone. Over the door in the centre is a small canopy, or possibly a signboard. The tithe map of 1838 shows the 'smithy' still in position, and it is described in the schedule as a 'shop'; the house butted on to the house and premises of John Smith, butcher, which is not shown in the 1800 survey as the property belonged to Thomas Pig.

PLATE LXXV. X.69 JOHN CURTIS. HOUSE, SHOP AND GARDEN. *House 2″ long. Viewed from the south.*

A thatched 1½-storey cottage, with high parapet gables. The wall is flint, and there are dentellated quoins, presumably in brick, at the left end and around all the openings. There are shallow-arched brick lintels to all windows and doors, and the right-hand door is halved. No clue as to the nature of the 'shop' has been found, and by 1838 the building is described as cottages. There was a house of similar shape there in 1730. The present house incorporates the flint wall of X.69, and the fossil gable of the thatched roof is visible in the east wall. The sole door is now in the centre, but the scars of the three doors of 1800 remain. The roof has been raised, and there is now a stack in the centre of the house.

PLATE LXXVI. X.72. COTTAGE. *Total length of building 3⅛″. Viewed from the north-east (green).*

This looks like a double cottage, but it could be a small farmhouse of the seventeenth century, converted to labourers' cottages. The attached building could be a bakehouse or something similar. In 1730 a house of the same plan had Thomas Rawling as tenant. In 1838 it was still there, but occupied simply as a cottage. Nothing of X.72 is now apparent, but the fossil gable in the north end of the cottage with 'J.B. Barrack House 1880' (probably John Barrett, grocer, draper, and dealer) might belong to it.

PLATE LXXVII. Y.1. WILLIAM BANKS, SENIOR, TENANT. *Oval 5½″ × 3⅞″. Viewed from the south-east (road).*

The drawing distorts the relationship of house and farm buildings, but it is clear that the farmhouse is the building that stands at an angle of about 30° to the road, the same angle as is shown on the tithe map of 1838. On the map of 1730 the angle is wider, about 70°, practically the same as that of the present house and on the drawing. Y.1 is a substantial farmhouse with a dentellated cornice. There is an attic window in the right-hand gable; the ground-floor windows have shallow-arched heads of gauged brickwork, and all windows are latticed. The present house is not very like the house of 1800 except in its proportions; the small part of the south front that is not cement-rendered is brick, and there is a bay window of mid-nineteenth century appearance.

The barn on Y.1 has a porch. This is unique on barns illustrated in the survey although others not drawn (e.g. D.1, V.1, X.1) may have porches. No porch is shown on the map of 1730. There are high undivided double doors, and on either side of the porch is a lean-to range with small doors. Beyond is a weatherboarded barn with pantiled roof, and a small two-storeyed building stands between it and the house. The present barn is a flint building with brick dressings and additions; the lean-to on the left in Y.1 is still there and is flint, but the brick porch now has a roof sloping forward instead of the pitched roof of Y.1. The porch must be an eighteenth-century addition to an older barn. The weatherboarded barn has gone. Y.1 also has a boarded kennel in the yard, and the other small building might be an outside privy except for its prominent position in front of the house. Its size does not seem to fit the building in that position on Map XIV.

PLATE LXXVIII. Y.30. COTTAGE. *House and lean-to 1¼″ long. Viewed from the south-east.*

Thatched 1½-storey cottage. The stack has lined-out corners and must be of post-and-board construction. The front windows are drawn unusually high in relation to the door. The outshut is boarded, and has a stout lintel and post exposed. The curious little construction in the foreground is of posts and boards. It could be an unroofed kennel, the top of a shallow well, or a screen over a cesspit. There was a small building of similar shape to the house on the site in 1730 and also on the tithe map. The cottage on the site in 1985 has flint walls to about six feet above ground, but is not easily identifiable with Y.30.

PLATE LXXIX. Z.1. WILLIAM BANKS JUNIOR, TENANT. *Oval 5½″ × 3¼″. Viewed from the northwest (road).*

Farmhouse with gable stacks, casement windows, and a mid-wall string-course. Badeslade's map of 1730 shows a building of similar plan to the main range. Map XV shows that the attached range with the long roof extends to the full width of the main house. It is not on the map of 1730. There is a small central projection on the south side of the house on both maps. Map XV also shows the low building with the small square window is detached. In 1985 the narrow windows on either side of the central door are blocked, as is the left-hand doorway. At each end of the first floor is a tall blank window, similar in shape to the narrow windows on Z.1, and there is another on the ground floor at the right-hand end. The brickwork is colour-washed, so it is not possible to say if these blocked windows were always mere decorative blanks. They are not shown on the drawing. The string course has been hacked away. At the west end of the present house is a fossil gable of flint, the added top five or six feet being brick with tumbles. The east gable-end is entirely brick. The outshut at the left end of the house has gone, but the present house has a two-storey lean-to range at the back, probably added before 1838.

The large barn, partly hidden by the outshut, is shown on Map XV as of an elongated cruciform shape, exactly the same as it appears on the map of 1730. The drawing does not make clear whether or not the open three-bay cartshed is attached to the barn; if it is, it could form the thin northern range of the barn, and may have been demolished by 1838, when the barn appears much shorter. If it is not attached to the barn it must be attached to the low range on the left, which is a stable with two open bays or a double-door cartshed at its southern end. The present barn, of brick, has large doors between pilasters, dentellated cornice, and double hourglass airholes; but it is aligned east-west and is evidently after 1838, though not long after. The stable and cartshed ranges are not on the 1730 map and have been demolished. The large plot on the other side of the road from Z.1 held the rectory.

PLATE LXXX. a.1. COULSEY SAVORY, TENANT. *White Hall. Oval 5½″ × 3¼″. Viewed from the west.*

The house is the stubby L-shape in the smaller group of buildings. Neither the larger group nor the long narrow range to the north of the house is shown on the drawing. The main range has a hipped roof in Hill's 'slate' convention, but the colour is brownish pink instead of grey. There are large sash windows of twelve panes. The lower range has a pantiled roof, and its upstairs windows stand alone in the survey in having prominent sills. The two ground-floor windows are of six square lights, also unique, and the left hand window has a large swinging shutter. The central porch has a flat roof and a curious chevron-headed doorway, perhaps an early attempt at Gothick. The imposing front range looks of the late-eighteenth century. The tithe map of 1845 shows the house in almost exactly the same form as on Map XVI, so the present 'Georgian' five-bay south front with its double roof and three-bay gable-end must be an early-Victorian addition at the west corner of the house of 1800. The cottage and stable range to the north of the house survive, and most of the farm buildings are still there, though altered and adapted. The best is the big brick barn with tumbles and a plain cornice, the most southerly building on Map XVI.

PLATE LXXXI. a.32. HOUSE. *Length 3¼″. Viewed from the south-east.*

This is a tall house of 2½ storeys. The gables may have barge-boards, and there are two underthatch dormers. The front has a straight joint, and the windows are a miscellaneous collection of casements and sashes. It seems quite possible that this is the last remnant of the manor-house of the Robsarts. They acquired the manor in the reign of Henry VII. Sir John Robsart (d.1552) lived at least the last part of his life at Stanfield Hall, near Wymondham, but it is likely that his daughter Anne or Amy (c.1532-60) lived at Syderstone after her marriage to Robert Dudley, later Earl of Leicester, in 1550. The map of 1720 shows a very long narrow building facing south-east and fronting the road represented on Map XVI by a dotted line. It stands some 200 yards north-north-east of the church — the same distance as a.32 — and, if we can rely on the scale, is about 270 feet long. There is a shallow projection at the back. Mrs Herbert Jones recorded in 1877 'traces of walls . . . village stories of two old elm trees which grew in front of the Hall, of remembrance of the floor of a room and a hearthstone, of ruins filled up, of the finding of candlesticks, fireirons, gold coins, pieces of carved brick in the 'Hall Lane' . . . the remains of extensive foundations near the church'. She located these remains in the 'large space of ground now occupied by the house and garden of Syderstone Rectory'.[95] The rectory was rebuilt in 1846, but the old rectory stood on the same site immediately north-west of the

[95]*Norf. Arch.* viii. 238-9.

160

church[96], so it seems likely that she misidentified the site. An estimate for repairs to estate cottages in 1829 describes the 'Old Farm House': 'In a dilapidated condition at present inhabited by six families whose situation is truly pitiable without convenience or comfort, although an extensive Building and capable of great Improvement'. The plan was to convert it into eleven tenements at a cost of £182.[97] This could have included both the larger buildings shown on Map XVI. Nothing is shown on the site on the 1845 tithe map, and in 1947 the Revd. Foudrinier recorded that it was pulled down 'it is said . . . a little over a hundred years ago'.[98] However, it must be admitted that, apart from the site and a certain tatty dignity, there is little to identify the house in the drawing with the hall of the Robsarts.

PLATE LXXXII.   b.1. NICHOLAS SAVORY, TENANT. *Up House Farm. Oval $5\frac{1}{2}'' \times 3\frac{3}{4}''$. Viewed from the east (road).*
On Map XVII this is the square building standing close to the road. The roof is pantiled, and all windows in the front, including the dormers, are latticed. There is a lean-to range of $1\frac{1}{2}$ storeys on the back with three windows, and there are two windows in the north gable-end. The house on the site on the map of 1720 is on the same alignment but is longer, and is probably represented by the fossil gable, in English bond brickwork, visible in the north end of the present house. The whole house seems to have been 'tarted up' somewhere in the middle of the nineteenth century — the windows have fluted corbels to the lintels, and a wooden string course has been tacked on between the ground and first floors.
There is a small open cartshed or dutch barn on the left of b.1. The large barn on Map XVII is not drawn, and seems to have been reduced in size by 1845, when two other large buildings appear at the eastern corner of the site. The farm buildings are now very dilapidated, and the barn is certainly not the building that was there in 1800.

PLATE LXXXIII.   b.29. COTTAGE. *House $2\frac{7}{8}''$ long. Viewed from the west (road).*
A cottage of $1\frac{1}{2}$ storeys, the left end of the roof half-hipped, the only positive appearance of this form in the survey. The right end is gabled, with a high parapet to protect the rough thatch. The projection in the centre, which is not shown on Map XVII, has the thatch carried down from the main roof, and could be a larder, bread oven, or shed/privy. If the cottage is divided the smaller lean-to serves the left half and must be entered from inside the house. A building of the same shape stands here on the 1720 map, and b.29 is certainly of the seventeenth century or earlier. A small modern housing estate stands on the site.

PLATE LXXXIV.   b.43. COTTAGE. *Length $3\frac{3}{4}''$. Viewed from the west (road).*
Map XVII shows only one building; the drawing does not make clear if the two buildings are joined, but both seem to be cottages, although there are no ground-floor windows in the right-hand building. Neither building is on the map of 1720, but they may have been acquired by the Walpoles after that date. The site now holds several nineteenth-century cottages.

PLATE LXXXV.   b.44. COTTAGE. *Length $3\frac{1}{8}''$. Viewed from the east (road).*
A double cottage of $1\frac{1}{2}$ storeys, although no upstairs windows are visible. The right end is marked as a different build by the hump in the thatch and the large vertical crack, although it will be noted that the crack passes through a long low window. The walls, in fact, are heavily cracked in both directions, suggesting timber-frame construction. A building of the same shape stood on the site in 1720, and indeed the house looks like a survival from the sixteenth century. The site is now occupied by a modern house.

[96]Houghton, Map 16.
[97]Houghton, M.7.p.
[98]NRO, MC 5/10.

NORFOLK RECORD SOCIETY

List of Publications

Report and Accounts for 1983

The following volumes have been published and are on sale at prices which will be quoted on application to the Hon. Secretary. Those marked with an asterisk are currently in stock: others can sometimes be obtained.

Vol. I	Calendar of Frere MSS: Hundred of Holt.
	Muster Roll, Hundred of North Greenhoe, circa 1523.
	Norwich subscriptions to the Voluntary Gift of 1662.
Vol. II	St. Benet of Holme, 1020-1210. The eleventh and twelfth century sections of Cott. MS. Galba E ii. The Register of the Abbey of St. Benet of Holme. Part I.
Vol. III	St. Benet of Holme, 1020-1210. Introductory Essay on the eleventh and twelfth century sections &c. Part II.
Vol. IV	The Visitation of Norfolk, 1664. Part I.
Vol. V	The Visitation of Norfolk, 1664. Part II.
Vol. VI	The Musters Returns for divers Hundreds in the County of Norfolk, 1569, 1572, 1574 and 1577. Part I.
Vol. VII	The Musters Returns for divers Hundreds in the County of Norfolk, 1569, 1572, 1574 and 1577. Part II.
Vol. VIII	A Norfolk Sessions Roll, 1394-1397.
	The Maritime Trade of the Port of Blakeney, Norfolk, 1587-1590.
	A Norfolk Poll List, 1702.
Vol. IX	Records of the Gild of St. George in Norwich, 1389-1547.
Vol. X	Norwich Consistory Court Depositions, 1499-1512 and 1518-1530.
Vol. XI	The First Register of Norwich Cathedral Priory.
Vol. XII	The Norfolk Portion of the Chartulary of the Priory of St. Pancras of Lewes.
Vol. XIII	East Anglian Pedigrees.
Vol. XIV	The Correspondence of Lady Katherine Paston, 1603-1627.
*Vol. XV	Minutes of Norwich Court of Mayoralty, 1630-1631.
Vol. XVI	Part I. Index of Wills Proved in the Consistory Court of Norwich, 1370-1550 (A to Hi).
	Part II. Index of Wills Proved in the Consistory Court of Norwich, 1370-1550 (Hi to Ro).
	Part III. Index of Wills Proved in the Consistory Court of Norwich, 1370-1550 (Ro to Z).
Vol. XVII	Post-Reformation Royal Arms in Norfolk Churches.
	Cellarer's Roll, Bromholm Priory, 1415-16.
	Subsidy Certificates, 1581.
Vol. XVIII	Bishop Redman's Visitation, 1597.
Vol. XIX	*Part I. Archdeaconry of Norwich: Inventory of Church Goods temp. Edward III.
	Part II. Archdeaconry of Norwich: Inventory of Church Goods temp. Edward III.
Vol. XX	The Knyvett Letters, 1620-1644.
Vol. XXI	Index of Wills Proved in the Consistory Court of Norwich, 1550-1603.
Vol. XXII	Baptisms in Church Book of Old Meeting House, Norwich, 1657-81.
	Baptisms and Deaths in Church Book of Gt. Yarmouth Independent Church, 1643-1705.
	Account Book of 'Baptised' Church in City of Norwich, 1726-45.
Vol. XXII contd.	Notes on Blomefield MSS. in Bodleian Library.
	Progress Notes of Warden Woodward relating to the Norfolk Property of New College, Oxford, 1659-1675.
*Vol. XXIII	The Freemen of Norwich, 1714-1752.
Vol. XXIV	Extracts from the two earliest Minute Books of the Dean & Chapter of Norwich Cathedral, 1566-1649.

REPORT OF THE COUNCIL FOR 1983

During the course of year we welcomed three new members, Dr. G. A. Metters, Mr. T. Mollard and the Folger Shakespeare Library in Washington. At the end of the year the number of subscribing members was 249.

After suffering considerable delays in the publication of our 1981 volume we are pleased to be able to report that it was finally completed and issued to members at the end of the year. At the same time the second volume in the series of Bacon Papers was issued as a double volume for 1982 and 1983. Our publication programme has therefore again been brought up-to-date.

The publication of the Bacon volume was the occasion of a reception at the University of East Anglia given jointly by the Society and the Centre of East Anglian Studies. Although the Society has not traditionally arranged meetings of its members, having regard to the activities of the Norfolk & Norwich Archaeological Society and other local organisations, the Council hopes that it may be able to arrange from time to time opportunities for members to meet together.

A general meeting of the Society was held during the year. The President, Officers and members of the Council of the Society were re-elected, and Professor J. R. Jones of the School of English and American Studies of the University of East Anglia was elected as an additional member of the Council, thus further strengthening the close relationship between the Society and the University.

M. V. B. RIVIERE
Chairman

THE NORFOLK RECORD SOCIETY

Income and Expenditure Account
for the year ended 31st December 1983

	1983 £	1983 £	1982 £	1982 £
INCOME				
Subscriptions	1,987			1,509
Sale of Publications	596		341	
Grant	200		200	
Donations	—		26	
Interest: Treasury Stock	84		84	
Savings Bank	362	446	441	525
Tax Refund — Covenants	30		44	
Royalties	27		—	
Overprovision for Volume 47		976		
		3,286		3,621
EXPENDITURE				
Provision for Printing and Despatch of Volumes 48 and 49	3,642		1,500	
Postage and Sundries	159		200	
Subscriptions	27		24	
Book Purchases	—	3,828	105	1,829
(Deficit)/Surplus for Year		£(542)		£1,792

Balance Sheet
as at 31st December 1983

	1983 £	1983 £	1982 £	1982 £
Accumulated Fund:				
Balance at 1.1.83		5,699		3,907
Deficit for Year (1982 Surplus)		(542)		1,792
Balance at 31.12.83		£5,157		£5,699
Represented by:				
Assets:				
£934.05 9% Treasury Stock (Cost)		649		649
Debtors:				
Subscriptions	645		532	
Income Tax	38		95	
Sales	401		63	
Grant	200	1,284	—	690
Cash at Bank:				
Barclays	2,774		529	
Trustee Savings Bank	5,862	8,636	5,417	5,946
		10,569		7,285
Less:				
Subscriptions in Advance	270		86	
Provision for Printing and Despatch of Volumes 48 and 49	5,142	5,412	1,500	1,586
		£5,157		£5,699

We have examined the foregoing Accounts and certify them to be in accordance with the books and vouchers of the Society.

NORWICH
5th OCTOBER 1984

PEAT, MARWICK, MITCHELL & CO.
Chartered Accountants